D1487330

PREACHING the Wedding SERMON

PREACHING the Wedding SERMON

SUSAN K. HEDAHL

Chalice Press
St. Louis, Missouri

© Copyright 1999 by Susan K. Hedahl

All rights reserved. No part of this book may be reproduced without written permission from Chalice Press, P.O. Box 179, St. Louis, MO 63166-0179.

All Bible quotations, unless otherwise noted, are from the *New Revised Standard Version Bible*, copyright 1989, Division of Christian Education of the National Council of the Churches of Christ in the United States of America. Used by permission. All rights reserved.

The poem "For the Time Being," section "Flight into Egypt," is from *W. H. Auden: Collected Poems*, edited by Edward Mendelson. Copyright 1944 and renewed 1972 by W. H. Auden. Reprinted by permission of Random House, Inc. All rights reserved.

Sermon by Walter J. Burghardt, S. J., is reprinted by permission from "Christ and/ or Buddha?" in *When Christ Meets Christ* (New York/Mahwah: Paulist Press, 1993), 98–102.

Quotes from Catullus are reprinted by permission of the publishers and the Loeb Classical Library from CATULLUS, translated by F. W. Cornish, revised by G. P. Goold, Cambridge, Mass.: Harvard University Press, 1913, revisions 1988.

Cover art: Christine Renna Thulin
Cover design: Michael A. Domínguez
Art direction: Michael Domínguez
Interior design: Wynn Younker

This book is printed on acid-free, recycled paper.

Visit Chalice Press on the World Wide Web at
www.chalicepress.com

10 9 8 7 6 5 4 3 2 1   99   00   01   02   03

Library of Congress Cataloging–in–Publication Data

Hedahl, Susan K. (Susan Karen)
    Preaching the wedding sermon / by Susan K. Hedahl.
        p.   cm.
    Includes bibliographical references and index.
    ISBN 0-8272-2960-7
    1. Preaching. 2. Wedding sermons. 3. Sermons, American. I. Title.
BV4278 .H43   1999
251'.1 — dc21   99-050581
                                                          CIP

Printed in the United States of America

He is the Way.
Follow Him through the Land of Unlikeness;
You will see rare beasts, and have unique
                adventures.

He is the Truth.
Seek Him in the Kingdom of Anxiety;
You will come to a great city that has expected
                your return for years.

He is the life.
Love Him in the World of the Flesh;
And at your marriage all its occasions shall
                dance for joy.

W. H. Auden, "For the Time Being,"
in *Collected Longer Poems*
(New York: Vintage Books, 1975), 196–97.

Contents

Preface

Why a book on preaching the wedding sermon? The question has several answers. First, it is the one area of occasional sermon preaching that offers the fewest available resources to ministers. While there are numerous wedding manuals that discuss the planning of the entire wedding service, the preaching itself is generally referred to only in a tangential way. Why is this? Given the unique aspects of every wedding, a minister's decision to preach at them is necessarily idiosyncratic. It is a homiletical area of work that is often without guidelines or precedents and, therefore, usually without resources.

Many personal and public factors contribute to conducting a marriage service, such as where it is held, which couples are eligible for marriage, the governance of a church's worship committee, and pastoral preferences related to whether there will even be proclamation. Certainly, the rubrics that focus on Sunday preaching or occasional preaching, such as at funerals, are generally absent in the arena of wedding proclamation. A decision to preach at one wedding may not hold true for another. This resource is a response to the wide array of proclamatory decisions a pastor confronts when discerning what is appropriate for a given wedding.

The need for a wedding sermon resource has also evolved out of my experiences as a homiletics instructor at Gettysburg Lutheran Theological Seminary. Beyond the occasional article, no materials currently exist for students interested in learning about the genre of wedding proclamation. And yet, outside of Sunday proclamation, it will be a type of preaching they will most often encounter in their ministries.

Furthermore, as a Lutheran parish pastor for a number of years, I became intrigued by the variety, rationale, and proclamation of wedding sermons. What *is* this kind of preaching anyway? I found myself simultaneously amused and frustrated as I created my own wedding sermons. Further studies in the areas of classical rhetorical and historical homiletics provided some answers for me about the origins of contemporary forms of the wedding sermon. The ancient Greeks and Romans always seemed to have "been there first," and in the case of wedding discourse, this has proven delightfully so. In fact, earlier classical sources reveal much deeper refinements in wedding discourse than we yet dare contemplate.

Readers of this volume will note the wide array of references to people and preaching of many times and places. The treasures of historical preaching are infrequently tapped, and it remains our loss that this is so. Valuable perspectives on humanity are not time-bound, and selections from different sources in this book prove that this is so.

Above all else, one of the most pervasive, though sometimes subtle, influences on this work are those marriages—current and past—I have encountered in my daily life that witness in countless and loving ways to the incarnational truth and meaning of marriage to which this volume speaks.

In rhetorical studies over the centuries, students were taught to keep what are called "commonplace books," collections of useful thoughts, illustrations, and topics for future use in speeches. While this book certainly acts as a map for pondering and writing wedding sermons, it will have served its purpose well as a commonplace book if a word, a topic, or a phrase elicits for the reader an idea for that "just right" wedding sermon.

Acknowledgments

Many people saw to it that this book was written in an informed and accurate manner.

My gratitude and thanks go to Richard L. Thulin, recently retired dean of Gettysburg Lutheran Theological Seminary and also my colleague in the field of homiletics. His unfailing good humor and encouragement for this project are typical of the support he has given to all my ventures.

A number of colleagues on the Gettysburg Lutheran Seminary faculty acted as readers for this book, and others offered assistance in varying ways: Drs. J. Paul Balas, Frances Taylor Gench, Scott Hendrix, and Norma Schweitzer Wood, and Drs. Herbert W. Stroup, Jr., and Herman Stuempfle, professors emeriti. Other contributors include Pastor Sheri Delvin, the Reverend Dr. Lucy Lind Hogan, Fr. Walter J. Burghardt, S. J., and the Reverend Dr. W. Sibley Towner. Thank you, as well, to those "Anonymous" whose contributions figure herein.

Sara Mummert, head reference librarian of our seminary library, showed almost miraculous powers and exquisite patience in locating needed resources. Andy Crouse, Kari Olsen, Piper Spencer, and Lisa Teichmann worked on this manuscript and rescued me from the vicissitudes of my new computer more times then I can count. Thank you.

Some Gettysburg ministers shared information on their denomination's perspectives on the wedding service—Father Hilbert of St. Francis Xavier Church, Dr. Jerry Dixon of

Memorial Baptist Church, the Reverend Louis Nyiri of First Presbyterian Church. the Reverend William Gettins gave me a Methodist perspective to think about. Thanks to ELCA Pastor Douglas Johnson for his helpful input and David von Schlichten for his assistance with the first appendix in this volume.

An alert group of scholars on an Internet list, "H-Rhetor," offered me some superlative new resources regarding Greek and Roman sources.

My students over the years in the preaching course "Wedding and Funeral Sermons" are largely responsible for many reflections in this work, as are the years I spent in parish ministry.

And of course, thank you to all of those people in my own life, professionally and personally, who have given me more than enough to ponder concerning this peculiar relationship called marriage!

1

Wedding Proclamation: What Is It?

Kingdom Come, by Amlin Gray, is a recent stage adaptation of Ole Rolvaag's pioneer epic, *Giants in the Earth*.[1] One early scene in the play features a grim-faced, stern Norwegian pastor officiating at the wedding of an upset, frightened couple. The woman is pregnant, the bearing of the pastor foreboding, and the groom tense. The only wedding discourse heard is that of the pastor, and he is angry. Indeed, the atmosphere is contrary to everything normally anticipated on the occasion of a wedding.

So exactly what discourse *do* we expect from clergy at weddings—specifically in terms of proclamation? What are its sources, its authority, its assumptions and proposals? Who is included or excluded? What is to be the tone of the sermon? What text or texts, scriptural and otherwise, does it draw on? How are the sermon topics chosen? To whom is it addressed? Do we expect anything at all?

---

[1]Amlin Gray, *Kingdom Come* (New York: Theatre Communications Group, 1983), 1.11–1.15. The play is based on Ole Rolvaag's *Giants in the Earth* (San Francisco: Harper Collins, 1965).

The most basic of all questions about the wedding sermon, heard from the concerned and the more cavalier, is: Why preach it if the marriage service doesn't require it?

Of all the types of occasional sermons a minister creates, the one most uniquely fashioned to the occasion is the wedding sermon. Its place, time, location in the service, and audience are unique and nonrepeatable events. Its address is multifaceted. Indeed, it can speak to several audiences simultaneously. It does not share the common features of liturgical repetition such as those found in the rhythms of Sunday preaching. Nor does it assume a commonly held human reality for all present, such as that of death, and the way its communal significance is voiced through the funeral sermon. *There is no agreed-upon wedding sermon prototype to which clergy may turn for homiletical models.* Collections of wedding sermons are sparse compared with those of other types of proclamation.

The very terminology used to describe wedding preaching is flexible. Lutherans note that "an address may follow [the scripture readings]."[2] Roman Catholics provide ample directions and call the preaching a "homily."[3] Presbyterians direct that "a brief sermon may be given."[4] Episcopalians suggest that "a homily or other response to the readings may follow."[5] Methodists say, "a sermon or other witness to Christian marriage is given."[6]

Other terms that are used for wedding proclamation are *message, meditation, thoughts on marriage, reflections, sermon,* and *homily.* These will be used interchangeably in this book, although each has its own liturgical and homiletical history. In similar fashion, those who preach wedding sermons will be

---

[2]*Lutheran Book of Worship* (Minneapolis: Augsburg Fortress Publishing; Philadelphia: Board of Publication, Lutheran Church in America, 1978), 202.

[3]*The Rites of the Catholic Church,* vol. 1. (New York: Pueblo Publishing, 1976), 725.

[4]*Book of Common Worship* (Louisville: Westminster/John Knox Press, 1993), 887.

[5]*The Book of Common Prayer* (New York: The Church Hymnal Coorperation and Seabury Press, 1979), 426.

[6]*The Book of Services,* The United Methodist Church (Nashville: The United Methodist Publishing House, 1985), 66.

variously designated as pastor, minister, preacher, proclaimer, and priest.

My classroom experiences with the wedding sermon reveal that students structure their wedding sermons on what they have heard in the past. The models have been less than helpful and sometimes result in "three points and a [bad nineteenth-century] poem."

Much homiletical reflection on marriage tends toward general cultural observations about marriage rather than offering any sound theological sustenance. Theologies of love and marriage are hazy at best. Stereotypes of female and male relationships are refracted through the lenses of wishful thinking, inexperience, and misunderstandings of human community. Text choices sometimes result in strange bedfellows theologically!

All of this is perfectly understandable when one considers the various views of marriage held both theoretically and in actuality. Statements vary widely: Marriage is social in nature. It is a spiritual and sacramental reality. It is not a sacrament but a civil contract. Romantic love is part of marriage. God's agape must be the basic gift in marriage. Marriage is a societal, practical means of maintaining the social order. Some view it as a mystical reflection of God's workings in the world.

Marriages can be arranged, freely chosen, carelessly entered into, or, in some cases, forced. The wedding may generate a panoply of emotions, with a range as broad as that which a funeral can elicit. Obviously, from the historical record, marriage is capable of being interpreted legitimately in many theological and nontheological ways.

Regardless of denominational faith perspectives, there is no normative approach to the wedding sermon. Some clergy preach in formulaic fashion: The same sermon is given at all weddings, with or without a scriptural basis. Others preach a form of premarital exhortation, sometimes moralistic in tone, addressing the do's and don'ts of married life. Preprinted materials, sometimes phrased according to denominational directives, are read, as are sermons purchased from the popular press or homily services. A few clergy dispense with the homily and witness only to the vows and the liturgical aspects of the ceremony. Others use an object lesson or a catchy mnemonic device—"Love is like…"

Any of these approaches can emerge as a result of tradition, historical precedent in a given locale, time constraints, pressures from the parish or marrying couple, the mixed theological makeup of the congregation, or clerical laziness—"After all, no one listens to anything on that day anyway…"

Given the plethora of views on marriage and the strange uniqueness of wedding sermons, is it even possible to write a book on them? Are there any points of commonality cross-denominationally? theologically? homiletically? What might serve as a plumb line for writing wedding sermons? What does this mean for the parish minister preaching at weddings?

The response to these questions is that this book is written with the conviction that *the Word of God, scripturally based, has a definitive place in the wedding ceremony. It publicly proclaims, through texts and topics, a theology of marriage to an assembly who may give a new hearing to what they are witnessing and enacting.* This assertion has a number of key phrases: *Word of God, texts, topics,* and *theology of marriage.* Taken together, they form the contents of this book.

First, the term *Word of God*, used as descriptive of the Bible in part or as a whole, is understood to provide the basic source for wedding proclamation. It is impossible to overestimate the importance of scriptural preaching at such a crucial juncture of choice and decision for two individuals and their communities. Rather than encourage the prevailing attitude that no one cares about the wedding proclamation, the basic premise of this book is that there are those who do care, and it is a pastoral responsibility to care professionally and personally and to care on behalf of others by offering sound wedding preaching.

The wedding sermon should offer a scriptural and theological lens through which to view the couple *and* the entire community—regardless of the status or roles of individual hearers within that community. Marriage is an event with community implications regardless of how many people attend the actual ceremony.

In this view, scripture is not merely a mantralike reading of the popular "love text" from 1 Corinthians 13 or the "Entreat me not to leave thee!" sentiments expressed in the book of Ruth. A mere repetition of historical texts lacking in contemporary contextualization is insufficient. Scripture is far more than a sentimental echoing of the experience of love with a cultural overlay.

Second, the *genre* of the wedding sermon, a type of occasional described in this book, is defined as *a strongly scripturally based proclamation inclusive of a skillful blending of topics*. While text choice may be the slightly easier of two realities, often suggested by denominations, the *choice of topics* for the borderlands of the twenty-first century offers overwhelming possibilities: views of the family, sexuality, love and its many meanings, the presence and role of the church, community relationships and the couple, issues related to interdenominational-, interfaith-, and nonfaith-based marriages.

Finally, a well-crafted wedding proclamation discerns and lifts up a *theology of marriage*. This emerges from the variable mix of couple, circumstances, individual pastoral theology, and denominational context. Since a wedding sermon reflects and bears the specific theological tradition from which it emerges in part or in whole, it is necessary to speak of a *proclamatory direction* marked by a particular theology of marriage. The homiletical faithfulness in a wedding sermon to which the minister is called is the theology of marriage from the faith tradition out of which that minister speaks. However, pastoral differences with the proclamatory direction focused by the person's denominational affiliation are possible; these are discussed later.

Clergy are responsible certainly for many types of speech related to a wedding: premarital counseling, service arrangements, the welcome, liturgical leadership, and witnessing to the couple's vows. Each of these areas offers written resources that can be used as references by the pastor and couple for the wedding homily.[7] Many of them are quite specific in relationship to denominational and psychological understandings of relationship. All clerical discourse expected around and during weddings will be considered in relationship to the primary focus of this book—the homiletical proclamation of a biblically based and proclaimed theology of marriage emerging from antecedent discussions among clergy, couple, and other participants. Some traditions view this task as essential and central, while others see it as merely peripheral. This volume will emphasize the importance of the former.

In order to understand the history, development, and manifestations of the wedding sermon, the text is arranged in this fashion. Chapter 2, "The Origins of Wedding Speeches," looks at the early classical forerunners of the wedding sermon from both ancient Greek and Roman sources. Most importantly, it examines the historical common grounds for the basis of this book, the analysis and construction of the wedding sermon vis-à-vis the classical rhetorical use of "topics" (traditionally known as *loci* or *topoi*).

Chapter 3, "The History of the Christian Wedding Sermon," describes the evolution of wedding proclamation in the Christian faith. Sermon excerpts demonstrate the continuity of a cluster of major faith topics through the centuries as well as the eclipsing or disappearance of others.

Chapter 4, "Choosing Texts for the Wedding Sermon," features the complexities of text choice in three ways: first, the choice of biblical texts for proclamation; second, the use of extrabiblical texts as part of the sermon (poems, letters, personal works); and finally, the use and abuse of biblical texts in proclaiming various theologies of marriage.

[7]See appendix B.

Chapter 5, "Choosing Topics for the Wedding Sermon," takes up the possibilities of topics, both scripturally based and otherwise, which are part of wedding proclamation. While the history of wedding topics has remained fairly stable over the centuries in many settings, Christian wedding proclamation has added others. Some of these include covenant/partnership, God's promises and human commitments, the cruciform shape of marriage, marriage as ministry and vocation, new beginnings, and the role of memory, grace, and forgiveness—to name only a few.

Chapter 6, "A Theology of Marriage in Context," discusses some of the social realities represented by those wishing to marry, such as divorce with remarriage, remarriage after the death of a spouse, issues related to children, denominational demands, interfaith and interracial/intercultural marriages, and special circumstances. In turn these societal configurations will be related to suggestions for combinations of texts, topics, and context that might form a given theology of marriage in proclamation.

Chapter 7, "Wedding Sermon Structures and Delivery," details a variety of possible sermonic forms that can lend shape to the various combinations of texts, topic choices, and extrabiblical materials. The chapter offers suggestions to the preacher for bringing the completed sermon to public delivery and some of the issues attendant upon that.

Chapter 8, " 'With Love': Sample Wedding Sermons," features a selection of present-day wedding proclamations in order to give the reader a sense of the multiplicity and commonality of sermonic approaches to marriage.

Historical research and contemporary custom offer many other possibilities for proclamation related to weddings and ceremonies of commitment that are not included in this book. These include those theologies of marriage that implicitly denigrate women, do not take into consideration the realities of divorce and remarriage, or offer religious or communal alternatives to a strictly monogamous form of marriage.

Given the fluidity of ritual and the enormous number of faith configurations in contemporary society, this volume has chosen to focus specifically on the wedding sermon preached at Christian weddings within a heterosexual context.[8]

Finally, the scope of this book in some sense is only preliminary. The combinations of texts, topics, theologies of marriage, and couples potentially leave open the form of the wedding sermon in an almost endless fashion. However, there are discernible points of commonality for all preachers: wedding sermon history, both homiletical and theological; scripture; the historical continuity of wedding topics; and the general expectations and faith expectations that listeners bring to wedding proclamation.

So, while introductory in tone, this book is an invitation to the reader to explore the many creative possibilities in a genre of preaching that marks one of the most significant of human events on the horizon of possibility and promise.

---

[8]There is a growing corpus of materials related to same-sex unions. This liturgical/homiletical territory is in flux concerning descriptive terminology, theology, and resources. Denominational discussions are also ongoing over the place of same-sex unions in liturgical rituals of many churches. For those ministering in settings related to such ceremonies, the following resources are suggested for historical and contemporary information and additional bibliography: John Boswell, *Same Sex Unions in Premodern Europe* (New York: Villard Books/Random House, 1994); and Kittredge Cherry and Zalmon Sherwood, eds., *Equal Rites: Lesbian and Gay Worship, Ceremonies and Celebrations* (Louisville: Westminster John Knox Press, 1995).

2

The Origins of Wedding Speeches

Ancestry of the Wedding Sermon

The Christian wedding sermon is rooted in ancient Greek and Roman wedding poetry and prose. Tracing this history, however, is reminiscent of trying to find Lewis Carroll's Cheshire Cat! While there is continuous historical evidence of the wedding sermon, it is tied closely to the episodic appearance and disappearance of the marriage service in the history of the church. According to Joseph Martos, "Before the eleventh century there was no such thing as a Christian wedding ceremony, and throughout the Middle Ages there was no single church ritual for solemnizing marriages between Christians."[1]

Several historical realities present difficulties in tracing the development of this elusive preaching genre. Biblical and early church writings reiterate views of marriage in relationship to the duties and obligations of those already married, but almost no *liturgical* information is available from a specifically homiletical perspective.

---

[1]Joseph Martos, *Doors to the Sacred* (New York: Image Books, 1982), 399.

The most basic problem with locating wedding sermons or instructions on preparing them lies with the inaccessibility of these texts. For example, Gregory of Nazianzus, rhetorician and archbishop of Constantinople (328?–389? C.E.), composed the *Moral Oration #4,* "On the Indissolubility of Marriage."[2] This text remains untranslated from the original Greek despite its importance as a pastoral manual for the priesthood for Chrysostom and Gregory the Great. The same holds true for wedding sermon texts from the Medieval and Reformation periods. Few continental sermons have been translated for the English-reading public. This is a significant loss given some of the available collections.[3] Some sermons published in English are faithful to the spelling and grammatical usage of their era and thereby frustrate or limit contemporary readership. John Donne's sermons, published by the University of California Press over the last few decades, are an example of the retention of original text forms.[4]

However, beyond the obvious dearth of available texts, there are several other major barriers that have affected the availability and study of the wedding sermon, all of these contingent on the larger context of the wedding ceremony itself.

The first problematic center of discussion regarding marriage is *scriptural*. It is difficult to clearly answer the question, What does scripture say and mean about marriage? The view of marriage in the New Testament offers a sketchy picture of that institution. While Jesus referred to marriage in several places, neither Jesus nor his followers presented any specifically new law or theory regarding it. Jesus' comments on marriage emerge from the challenges presented to him regarding the divorce

---

[2]Gregory of Nazianzus, "The Indissolubility of Marriage," Fourth Moral Oration, ed. Migne, *Patrologiae Graecae*, vol. 37 (Paris: Migne, 1857), 521–753.

[3]Scott Hendrix, "Masculinity and Patriarchy in Reformation Germany," *Journal of the History of Ideas* 56:2 (1995): 177–93. See also Susan Karant-Nunn, "Kinder, Kuche, Kirche: Social Ideology in the Sermons of Johannes Mathesius," *Germania Illustrata: Essays on Modern German Presented to Gerald Strauss* (Kirksville, Mo.: Sixteenth Century Journal Publishers, 1992), 121–40.

[4]See the *Sermons of John Donne*, ed. George R. Potter and Evelyn M. Simpson, 10 vols. (Berkeley: University of California Press, 1991).

laws of his day. He refers his listeners back to the views of male and female in Genesis. In other words, for the faithful who marry, the rules and rituals attached to marriage emerge from the already determinative ancient faith foundations.

Jesus' other recorded comments, made when he was at a wedding in Cana, had nothing to do with the marriage but the provision of wine for the festivities. A later discussion with the pharisees over the woman with seven husbands and the question "Whose wife will she be at the Resurrection?"[5] elicited a remark hinting at a state of humanity in which there is no such thing as marriage at all.

In fact, many of Jesus' statements, as well as his lifestyle, have been interpreted as offering an alternative to married life. Later Pauline and apostolic comments on marriage added new metaphoric, poetic, theological, legal, and social dimensions to the reality of marriage.

Second, from a *politicohistorical perspective*, the wedding service has been considered for centuries a ceremony negotiable between the demands of both state and church. The wedding rituals related to the service that earlier Christians developed must be considered within the context of the prevailing Roman empire's history of wedding customs, based in part on inherited Grecian customs. These ranged from the *sponsalia,* the ceremony of betrothal, to the *nuptiae*, the actual marriage ceremony, which developed over centuries.[6] The background for these Roman views of marriage can be found in various state and canonical laws.

Throughout the development and spread of Christianity, tensions can be noted between the secular and religious codes established for believers. What indicated someone was married? Arguments included whether or not marriage was established through consent (e.g., privately or through a ceremony), the presence of sexual intercourse, or the role of property

---

[5]See Matthew 22: 25–28.

[6]See "Marriage," in James Hastings, ed., *Encyclopedia of Religion and Ethics*, vol. 3 (New York: Charles Scribner's Sons, 1916), 433–43.

exchanges and holdings. One example of this is the establishment of a marriage in Roman civil law through property ownership, while in later canon law marriage was seen as being established through a conjugal relationship.[7] This centuries-old oscillation between the differing views maintained by secular and religious authorities continues to this day with a variety of legal and theological responses and considerations involved.

In the author's state of Pennsylvania, for example, the stated code for who may officiate at weddings says:

> Marriage is in law a civil contract and does not require any particular form of solemnization before officers of church or state, but it must be evidenced by words in the present tense, uttered with a view and for the purpose of establishing the relation of husband and wife.[8]

This is buttressed by a list of court cases, dating from 1885 to 1975, that support the assertion that marriage is understood to be a social institution of the state.[9] Whatever the views of marriage ascertained by a given Christian faith perspective, the "state" (however that may be defined) continues to act as the regulatory overseer of marriage in most parts of the world, offering ceremonies sans sermon.

Next, from a contemporary rhetorical perspective, the genre of preaching called the wedding sermon is one that is only *occasional.* Unlike the somewhat predictable funeral sermon, or Sunday lectionary preaching, the wedding sermon is subject to several factors, which means that it can be highlighted or omitted completely. It is a "may" rubric, a fluctuating "extra" that the minister may or may not decide to include in a wedding

---

[7]E. Schillebeeckx, O. P., *Marriage: Human Reality and Saving Mystery* (New York: Sheed and Ward, 1965). This volume provides a superlative historical look at marriage from the Old and New Testaments to the post-Tridentine period. Scriptural, historical, and canonical references are abundant.

[8]From the Pennsylvania Law Code: 23 PA. C. S. A. #1305—"Marriage."

[9]Information provided by the Clerk of Courts, Adams County Courthouse, Gettysburg, PA, 17325.

ceremony. Ministers may omit it simply because they think the biblical and faith illiteracy of the parties involved merits that step, or their own views of weddings do not make it worth the pastor's time to proclaim a scriptural perspective.

Topics: The Historical Plumb Line

The question, What is a wedding sermon? continues to be problematic. Because of its occasional nature and specificity, it is difficult to identify models or outlines for this proclamatory genre. However, given its evolution, denominational theological perspectives, individual preachers' views, cultural-social realities in different eras, and the ancient rhetorical history in which it is couched, there is one central factor that does offer historical and analytical continuity among all these realities: It is what classical rhetoricians call *topoi*, *loci*, or "topics."

Over the centuries there is a remarkable consistency of topics in both pagan and Christian literature. Noting the similarities and dissimilarities of these topics in the following wedding sermon materials will provide the focus in the following chapters. These topics of marriage, with numerous variations, can be categorized under *Remembrances*, *Exhortations,* and *Blessings,* and, often in that order, form the structural core of wedding sermons past and present.

Remembrances include the couple, their courtship, love, and special attributes; the community; the role of parents, relatives, and friends in the lives of the couple; significant events that have resulted in the occasion of the wedding; remembrances of history related to family; the marriages of other notable people; the establishment of marriage by God or the gods; the role of a religious establishment or context of some sort; and the language of contracts/covenants/agreements—in some cases related to the dowry and property holdings.

Exhortations may form the topics and include admonitions to remember the difficulties, obligations, and responsibilities of married life and to preserve monogamy and avoid lust and adultery; the duties and obligations of each sex in the marriage state; the gift of virginity to the marriage; the stewardship of property and lands (in some cases related to the dowry); the fulfilling of duties to society and the surrounding community; the bearing, rearing, and education of children; the mutual support of husband and wife; and injunctions of faithfulness to God/the gods.

Blessings invoked for the future include expressed hopes for good health, happiness, children, longevity, the avoidance of harm, a long life, the support of others, and the invocation of the gods/God on the marriage.

The genre of the wedding sermon does have a discernible past-present-future structure from ancient to contemporary times, which is reflected to some extent in the topical content and structure of today's wedding sermon.

Greek and Roman Sources

Direct historical influences on the wedding sermon itself are based on ancient Greek and Roman sources, which include two major types of writing—poetry and prose. The former includes the writings of poets, satirists, and playwrights; the latter, handbooks on rhetorical instruction describing the genre of wedding speeches. In other words, ceremonial wedding discourses were recorded by the ancients in both literary and popular forms.

From ancient sources there are records of various genres of speeches, in prose or poetry form, written for such occasions as birthdays, going to or returning from war, funerals, athletic competitions, and the death of great persons. These forms of persuasive speaking are called *epideictic*, or variously, "display" or "praise-and-blame" oratory. Numerous Greek and Roman rhetoricians both practiced and instructed students in the art of these speech forms over the centuries. It is to these we turn in order to gain some background on the influences determining the structure and content of the ancient Christian wedding sermon.

Earliest Greek sources record fragments of popular and literary wedding songs in poetic form.[10] The unions of gods and goddesses were frequently used as theological prefaces to the rituals of marriage. The wedding of Peleus and Thetis, the god and goddess who were parents of Achilles, is an example of this that is mentioned in Homer's *Illiad* and repeated in other contexts.

The most significant ancient Greek writer to contribute to wedding discourse was the female poet Sappho (ca. 630 B.C.E.). Her work was a major precursor to later prose wedding service discourse. The 700 extant fragments of her poetry include such topics as congratulations for the couple, a lamentation for the loss of virginity, invocation of the gods of marriage, and praise for the songs of bridesmaids. The latter is translated in this fragment, titled "Bridesmaids' Carol 1":

O Bride brimful of
rosy little loves!

O brightest jewel
of the Queen of Paphos!

Come now
to your
bedroom to your bed
and play there
sweetly gently
with your bridegroom

And may Hesperus
lead you not at all

---

[10] These songs have been called *epithalamium,* which is defined this way: "Literally the word means 'at the nuptial chamber *thalmos* and initially it probably designated a kind of song sung at the door, or at the nuptial couch itself, just before the consummation of the union. By the time of Catullus, greatest of the Latin epithalamists, European poets had begun to call almost any wedding song or poem an epithalamium…" (from Virginia Tufte, *The Poetry of Marriage* [Los Angeles: Tinnon-Brown, 1970], 3).

unwilling
until
you stand wondering
before the silver

Throne of Hera
Queen of Marriage[11]

The early church did not live easily with Sappho's lush poetry; it considered it a form of competing sensuous discourse contrary to that of pulpit discourse. In approximately 380 C.E., Gregory of Nazianzus, curiously a superlative rhetorician of the classical order himself, ordered the burning of her works wherever found. In 1073, Pope Gregory VII ordered her writings burned publicly in Constantinople and Rome. Only in the Renaissance did Sappho's poetry surface again for appreciation and new insight into the works of a lyric poet who offers one of the first written records on actual marriage and wedding speeches.

Following Sappho in the seventh century B.C.E. and thereafter, Euripides and Aristophanes were among the better-known Greek playwrights to speak of marriage from a ceremonial perspective in their works.

A Roman poet, Gaius Valerius Catullus (84–54 B.C.E.), wrote two wedding songs in poetry form, #61 and #62. In these poems we read a description of the discourse attendant upon a wedding ceremony, in this case for that of a Manlius Torquatus and Vinia Aurunculeia.

In Poem #61, the sentiments are both exhortatory and lyrical at the same time. The god of marriage, Hymen, is invoked. The beauty and duties of the bride are discussed, the lures of the former unmarried state are dismissed and subject to the discipline of the married state, the power of the bridegroom is noted, and children are wished as a blessing upon the couple. The poem closes with an admonition to the listeners

---

[11] "#31 Bridesmaids Carol 1," *Sappho: A New Translation,* trans. Mary Barnard (Berkeley: University of California Press, 1962).

to leave the newlyweds to their privacy. An excerpt from the end of the poem describes their love and the generative power of marriage:

> Let him first count up the number of the dust of
>   Africa
> and of glittering stars, who would number
> the many thousands of your joys.
>
> Sport as ye will, and soon bring children forth.
> It is not fit that so old a name should be without
>   children,
> but that they should be ever born from the same
>   stock.[12]

Poem #62 is composed of a dialogue between young men and maidens invoking Hymen, the god of marriage, noting the gift of virginity as a gift to the marriage bed and concluding with an admonition to the bride to remember that her parents and her new husband all have a claim on her "maidenhead." A portion of the dialogue on the part of the young men reads:

> Hesperus, what more welcome fire than thine shines
>   in the sky?
> for thou with thy flame confirmest the contracted
>   espousals,
> which husbands and parents have promised
>   beforehand,
> but unite not till thy flame has arisen.
> What is given by the gods more desirable than the
>   fortunate hour?[13]

Besides poetry, rhetorical instruction manuals and treatises provide the other key sources for tracing the history of the wedding sermon. Sources of any length on wedding discourse

---

[12]"The Poems of Catullus LXI," from *Catallus Tibullus and Pervigilium Veneris* from the Loeb Classical Library collection. Trans. F. W. Cornish (Cambridge, Mass.: Harvard University Press. 1956), 85.

[13]Ibid., 87.

are few, but two major sources of rhetorical instruction are crucial to an understanding of the historical development of the wedding sermon. Each contains instructions as to both content and form of the speeches; these are the extant writings of Pseudo-Dionysius and Menander the Rhetor.

Pseudo-Dionysius' treatise *On Epideictic Speeches,*[14] probably written sometime between the third and fifth centuries B. C. E., notes two different types of wedding speeches: first "Part 2. Procedures for Marriage Speeches"' (*gamnlion*) and then "Part 4. Procedure for the Bridal-Chamber" (*epithalamios*).

In the former, the writer notes that "the subject of the desirability of marriage is set to young students for writing more often than other topics."[15] In outline form, this is what the writer suggests a speech should contain, beginning with the theological foundation of marriage:

> the topic based on the gods, viz., that they discovered and showed the way to marriage for mankind, for Zeus and Hera…, the first who joined and coupled; Zeus is called father of all, and Hera "Zyguia," from the joining of male with female, and it was from these divinities that the choir of the other gods came into life, those who are acclaimed at marriages and are called gods of marriage and birth.[16]

Dionysius then says that the next topic should relate to the generation of the species: "This one might call the fairest contribution…"[17] The benefits of marriage are the next topic to receive attention: "First, in reputation…Marriage is also of the greatest use in facing the pains and distresses of life …and…Feasts and celebrations are delightful because they take place in the company of many."[18]

---

[14]Pseudo-Dionysius, "On Epideictic Speeches," *Menander Rhetor* (Oxford: Clarendon Press, 1981), 362ff.

[15]Ibid., 366.

[16]Ibid.

[17]Ibid.

[18]Ibid.

Another topic follows, relating to famous historic marriages: a wish for good fortune in the marriage, for children, and "for the averting of misfortune."[19] The personalities of the partners and the merits of the family are also to be discussed, but arranged according to the noteworthiness of each.

Dionysius advises the bridegroom to praise the advantages of marriage just as he would his beloved, concluding that the style should be "simple…but occasionally raising the tone to one of dignity, if this is required by the thought."[20]

The other type of wedding-related discourse is covered in "Part 4. Procedure for the Bridal-Chamber Speech" (*epithalamios*). This was given at the door of the bridal chamber following the actual wedding. Dionysius says, "It naturally follows the marriage speech, and is indeed almost identical, except for the difference of time, since it is spoken at the conclusion of the marriage…There are some examples of this type in Sappho."[21]

In noting the history of the wedding songs, Dionysius tells the student writer to note the differences between prose and poetry: "In the prooemium [say that] 'others sing the hymneal song, we sing in prose instead, not with flutes or lyres or any such beauteous sound, but with praises and hymns honoring the newly married pair.'"[22] Following the same format, the writer says, "Let there be an exhortation to the married couple, to be fond of one another and live in concord as far as possible. Explain the blessings that are sure to follow."[23] He goes on to quote Homer to buttress his argument and then concludes that he hopes the couple may have children so [we] "have a subject for this sort of speech once again."[24]

In Menander the Rhetor, *Treatise II*, Part IV, "The Epithalamium," the author says, "The 'epithalamium' is called

---

[19]Ibid.
[20]Ibid., 368.
[21]Ibid., 370.
[22]Ibid.
[23]Ibid.
[24]Ibid., 371.

by some the wedding speech ('gamelios'). It is a speech which hymns bridal chambers and alcoves, bride and bridegroom, family, and above all the god of marriage himself. It delights in stories of charm and love, for these are germane to the subject."[25]

As far as the style of this speech, Menander steers a course between high style and a more relaxed form, offering suggestions for both but emphasizing the latter. In this version, the writer should note the history of the gods in relationship to marriage, written works hymning the god of marriage, something in praise of marriage, and then how the marriage was contracted or established.

This is followed with words about the respective families. Says Menander, "You should not dwell long on the topic of the family, for fear of being tediously long-winded, and also because the subject does not have this professed intention, but weddings and bridal alcoves."[26]

Other topics include the bridal pair followed by one topographical in nature— "the description of the bridal chamber and alcoves, and the gods of marriage."[27] He suggests addressing either Eros or the gods of marriage.

In Part VII of the treatise, "The Bedroom Speech" (*Kateunastikos*), Menander says, "The bedroom speech is a very brief one…the essential points…are those appropriate to the bridal chamber, the union of the couple, the alcoves, Cupids, hymeneal songs, and the rites of marriage."[28] Urging the speech writer to be "brief" with this genre is amusing since his instructions are more lengthy than those of the first type of wedding speech!

As far as the resources the speechmakers can draw on, Menander is aware of his primary heirs: "You should also quote from Sappho's love poems, from Homer, and from Hesiod,

---

[25]Ibid., 135.
[26]Ibid., 141.
[27]Ibid., 145.
[28]Ibid., 147.

who also said a great deal about unions and marriages of gods in his *Catalogues of Women*."[29]

He offers several possible topics but admonishes the speaker to choose only one or two and offers model sentences as "starters." "You should add: 'You will see delightful dream visions that prophesy the future to you with happy augury, children, lifelong harmony, increase of property, praiseworthy management of your wealth.'" [30]

The dual role of the wedding speaker is noted; both the couple and the celebrants should hear this: "Address yourself to the audience and say: 'While the couple themselves are celebrating the rites of marriage and being initiated, let us put on garlands of roses and violets, let us light torches and have sport around the chamber, let us start a dance and cry "Hymen!" beating the ground with our feet, clasping hands, all of us wearing garlands.'"[31]

The rest of the composition instructs attention to support of the male (primarily); praise of the season and the evening hour; exhortations concerning the past and the nature of the courtship; and the advantages of marriage; and concludes with prayers for the couple. "You should then argue…that the advantage of marriage lies in concord in the household and preservation and increase of wealth, and most important, in the procreation of children to follow on in the family, to be benefactors to their country, to organize festivals."[32]

The content of the entire speech, says Menander, will reflect that "grace and charm come not only from traditional stories and narrative but from plainness and simplicity in the speaker's personality. The speech should be unadorned and… in the manner of non-oratorical prose, the 'talk.'" [33]

---

[29]Ibid., 141.
[30]Ibid., 151.
[31]Ibid., 153.
[32]Ibid., 157.
[33]Ibid., 159.

Conclusion

The history of the Christian wedding sermon is located in classical Greek and Roman sources, both literary and popular. A reading of these sources demonstrates some of the potential and delightful resources that they offer to ministers today and provides a tested means of discourse that exhibits sound historical continuities.

Apart from following the forms of a biblical text, the matter of how to structure a wedding homily may be problematic for the preacher. The sources offer ample choices that relate to the form of wedding preaching, for example, the use of the threefold time structure or possibly the contemporary preacher's creativeness in composing or using good wedding poetry! Contemporary preaching, in regard to the former possibility, sometimes lacks the theological substance that is afforded by well-timed, thoughtful exhortation. The earlier sources also emphasize a variety of speech forms at weddings. Are there ways, for example, to involve other members in the community in speaking to the gathering apart from liturgical responses?

Other elements are apparent in the classical sources that can lend similar emphases to today's wedding proclamation. These are the spirit of celebration, especially that which emerges from community participation and the frankly incarnational approach to marriage. A contemporary sermon that can also capitalize on the aesthetics of the occasion, whether by form or by content, is a worthy goal for the preacher.

The common historical thread that links all eras of wedding discourse together are the "topics," also known in Greek and Roman as *topoi* and *loci*. These topics have played a prominent part over the centuries, giving speechmakers numerous possibilities for refining the wedding speech genre in a variety of specific ways. Given the basic nature of humanity in community, many of these topics are still important for today's wedding sermon and may well flesh out the activities of love in more concrete fashion.

One topical motif that runs through all the classical wedding discourses is that of connecting the couple's life to issues of theology and, specifically, divine presence. While this may be assumed in a Christian wedding sermon, the question should be asked nevertheless by the preacher, What is theological in nature about this wedding sermon, and how is God's presence in this upcoming marriage expressed to this couple in it? It also raises another issue of what the pastor preaches when the couple is either generally or avowedly agnostic in outlook. This becomes complicated when the couple are well known in the community or are relatives of the minister. There is no easy answer except that the definition of a "Christian sermon" is reframed in relationship to the pastor's definitions of pastoral care as well as homiletical theology.

In general, the available classical sources for the wedding sermon offer a strong case for their use, at least in part, as models and sources of contemporary wedding proclamation!

3

The History of the Christian Wedding Sermon

Documentation of the wedding sermon, in both praxis and theory, is sketchy at best in the Christian era. While the early church said a great deal about the duties and responsibilities of marriage, some of it is extremely sexist and misogynistic, and little is available concerning the actual liturgical-homiletical forms of discourse used to express these. Furthermore, it is impossible to know if some of the extant sermon fragments and sermons on marriage were actually delivered at weddings. Evidence is not conclusive either way in many cases. However, dubious texts may be considered, at least as tangential evidence, for reflecting the key concerns and topics that preachers emphasized for the engaged and the married at a given historical time. Sometimes a sermon text was repeated on many different occasions. Other sermons were preached in settings that were not their original context—for example, exegetical works of the Patristic Era read as sermons.

In order to trace some of the common topical threads in Christian wedding proclamation, the following is offered as a representative sampling of sermons from early sources to the end of the nineteenth century. What is significant about early evidence of wedding ceremony discourse is the continuity of the topics compared with those of the pre-Christian era. The core set remains more or less the same, with the added weight of a primary scriptural touchstone and the substitution of the pantheon and history of the gods with the God of Jesus Christ. Additionally, it is possible to trace new secondary developments in theologies of marriage.

Certain core perspectives and assumptions nuance Christian views of marriage as they are reflected in such wedding preaching topics. First, marriage is considered from the perspective of monogamy. Second, divorce is forbidden, since marriage is exclusive through time. Third, the view of women and women's roles is considerably elevated, considering historical perspectives, although what this "elevation" means shifts over time and needs definition. Fourth, Paul's analogy of the mystical union of Christ and his church with marriage adds a significant dimension to the sanctity of marriage and a new root metaphor to Christian thinking on marriage. Fifth, the eschatological note is evident in many sermons as the preacher bases it on the story of the wedding feast of the Lamb in Revelation. It is possible to speculate that the diminution of this particular topic over the centuries may correlate with the rise in life expectancy and the drop in mortality rates in many places. Sixth, the development of textual interpretative techniques over the centuries built up a variety of interpretations regarding texts from the Song of Songs and other wisdom literature.

Finally, sexuality is considered (and variably described) both a gift of the marriage and a potential source of its spiritual ruination. Such tensions are absent from the classical texts at a religious level. Much of the earliest preaching reflects a catastrophic view of marriage in this regard, particularly in contrast to competing views of celibacy and spirituality. Alternative forms of sexual expression or restraint, lawful or unlawful, are a pronounced theological counterpoint running throughout the centuries of wedding proclamation.

The following is a selection of some translated texts by notable theologians from the second through the nineteenth centuries, which affords some insight into the topics and perspectives held by different preachers at different times.

Three realities mark these texts. First, the voice of proclamation and commentary on marriage through the centuries is male. The views of women on marriage are absent, and one wonders what set of topics would have emerged had female reflections found voice in proclamation.[1] Next, it is important to note the topical affinities assorted preachers shared and, finally, the ways in which Christian preachers mirrored so many of the topics present or suggested in ancient classical wedding literature. Sappho's name is acknowledged in several different contexts.

One of the earliest complete sermons on the topic of marriage is from the homily on marriage by Origen (185–254 C.E.). A master of the allegorical form of interpretation, he left a rich and long record of sermonic discourse on biblical texts. The homily is based on Song of Solomon 1:1–12. Says Origen of this text in the sermon, "This is the character in this book, which is at once a drama and a marriage song. And it is from this book, that the heathen appropriated the epithalamium, and here is the source of this type of poem; for it is obviously a marriage-song that we have in the Song of Songs."[2]

The entire homily is devoted to an allegorizing of this book in relationship to the spiritual marriage between the soul and Christ, "the Bride made perfect in the House of the Bridegroom."[3]

---

[1] Although not from the pulpit, female commentary on marriage was present in other ways. Examples of this are found in the writings of female mystics. Pithy commentary abounds in such reflections as those of the wife of Bath in Chaucer's *Canterbury Tales*. For more information on the reflections of women in male preaching, see "Women and Preaching in the Patristic Age," in David G. Hunter, ed., *Preaching in the Patristic Age: Studies in Honor of Walter J. Burghardt, S.J.* (New York: Paulist Press, 1989), 53–72.

[2] Origen, "The First Homily," *20 Centuries of Great Preaching* (Waco: Word Books, 1971), 39. Originally published in Frederick W. Farrar, *Lives of the Fathers* (New York: Macmillan, 1889), 291–92.

[3] Ibid., 48.

From a later date come some sermon materials of Augustine (354–430 C.E.) on marriage. The date of the fragment is unknown. Whether this is an excerpt from an actual wedding sermon can only be guessed at. In a short space, it reveals several key topics typical of early Christian-Era thinking on marriage, topics to which Augustine returned repeatedly.

> Let whosoever can receive this, receive it (Mt. 19:12) [the gift of celibacy]. "But I can't," he says. You can't? "No, I can't." To your aid there comes a particular authority from the apostle, to feed you on milk, to the effect that *if they cannot practice continence, let them marry.* Let something be done, in order to obtain indulgence. The function of indulgence is to save you from landing in eternal punishment. Let what is lawful be done, in order to be pardoned for what is not lawful. He indicates this by what comes next: I prefer them to marry, rather than to burn (1 Cor. 7:9). He made a concession, I'm saying, to incontinence, because he feared something worse; he feared eternal pains, he feared what's awaiting, what's in store for adulterers. Even the fact that married couples, overcome by desire, make use of their conjugal rights more than is necessary for having children, I place among the things for which we say every day, *Forgive us our debts, as we too forgive our debtors* (Mt. 6:12).[4]

Sermons on the wedded life were not confined simply to marriage; comments on marriage found their way into some interesting settings. Bernard of Clairveaux preached a sermon on 1 Timothy 1:5 ("love that comes from a pure heart, a good conscience, and sincere faith") before the Cistercian abbots assembled at Citeaux, the mother house of the order. His sermon is titled "On the Three Ways to Heaven Followed By Three Classes of Christians." He says of those married:

---

[4]Augustine, "Sermons," *The Works of Saint Augustine: A Translation for the 21st Century*, III/10, trans. and notes Edmund Hill, O. P., ed. John E. Rotelle, O.S.A. (New York: New City Press, 1995), 164.

As for the third order, that, namely, of married persons, it is not necessary to dwell at length upon it, as it does not particularly concern us. It consists of those who for the most part cross the wide sea of this world by fording, having beyond doubt a difficult and dangerous, yea, and a very long road to traverse, inasmuch as they can make no "shortcuts." The danger of this road is manifest from the fact that so many, to our sorrow, seem to perish in it, whilst only very few appear to complete the journey by that way without mishap. For it is a very difficult matter, particularly in our own times, when malice so much abounds, to avoid the whirlpools of passion and the gulfs of deadly sin amidst the wild waves of the world's restless ocean. [5]

From the sixteenth century comes a sermon preached by Martin Luther at the marriage of Sigismund von Lindau in 1545. He uses several scriptural texts and begins with the history of marriage based on the Genesis narrative. He notes three types of people—those who should marry but do not, those who do not need to, and those who can and will. He contradicts some of the notions of celibacy of his time by reassuring the couple: "For here God says to the man: You are my man; and to the woman: You are my woman. And because I know that God speaks so to me, I also know that all the angels speak so to me, and love me and respect me."[6]

On having children: "Then, if our dear God and Father in heaven grants children…you will be doing right and performing better and nobler good works than all the monks and nuns; then you will be living in God's vocation and ordinance." [7]

Luther considers the dangers of adultery and bearing children out of wedlock and concludes with an oft-repeated topic on marriage as a vocation: "But it is also required that every

---

[5]Bernard of Clairveaux, *St. Bernard's Sermons,* trans. by a priest of Mount Melleray, vol. 3 (Westminster, Md.: Carroll Press, 1950), 307.

[6]Martin Luther, *Luther's Works, Sermons I,* ed. and trans. John Doberstein (Philadelphia: Muhlenberg Press, 1959), 360.

[7]Ibid., 363.

Christian should remain in the estate and calling in which he has been placed by God and faithfully discharge its duties; then God adds felicity and blessing."[8]

One of John Donne's (1573–1631) wedding sermons picks up the early patristic topic of the relationship between the spiritual and earthly aspects of marriage and weaves them together to form the structure of the sermon. His text is Hosea 2: 19, Bishop's Bible: "and I will marry thee unto me forever." "First, a secular marriage in Paradise; secondly, a spirituall marriage in the Church; and thirdly, an eternall marriage in heaven."[9]

Donne also includes the topics of threats to the state of marriage as adduced from various heresies throughout history. He also considers the theological differences between Catholicism and the faith in England on marriage. "If it be a Sacrament, who administers it, who is the Priest? They are fain to answer, the Bridegroom and the Bride, he and she are the Priest in that Sacrament. As mariage is a civill Contract, it must so be done in publick."[10]

The wedding is finally cast into an apocalyptic framework in the latter part, reinforced by quotes from Revelation. After detailing Christ's marriage to each individual soul, Donne claims that the wedding at which he now officiates is to be considered this way:

> And in the mean time bless these thy servants, with making this secular marriage a type of the spirituall, and the spirituall an earnest of that eternall, which they and we, by thy mercy, shall have in the Kingdome which thy Son our Saviour hath purchased with the inestimable price of his incorruptible blood.[11]

One of the best-known pastoral figures of seventeenth-century England is Jeremy Taylor. His sermon "The Marriage

---

[8]Ibid., 367.

[9]John Donne, *The Sermons of John Donne,* ed. Evelyn M. Simpson and George R. Potter, vol. 3. (Berkeley: University of California Press, 1957), 241–42.

[10]Ibid., 243.

[11]Ibid., 255.

Ring" begins with the history of marriage and then focuses primarily on the rights and duties of marriage. The sermon is gentle but direct in tone and forthright in its insights about the problems inherent in the married state.

> Let them be sure to abstain from all those things which by experience and observation they find to be contrary to each other. They that govern elephants never appear before them in white, and the masters of bulls keep from them all garments of blood and scarlet, as knowing that they will be impatient of civil usages when their natures are provoked by their proper antipathies. Let the husband and wife infinitely avoid a curious distinction of mine and thine for this hath caused all laws, and all the suits, and all the wars in the world; let them have but one person, have also but one interest.[12]

From the eighteenth century comes a fascinating piece by John Wesley (1703–1791) titled "A Thought Upon Marriage." This was done in Lisburn on June 11, 1785, and while the context is not clear, the piece could have easily been addressed to those intending to marry. In it he recapitulates the history of the wedding sermon by posing his faith questions counter to that of Sappho's works.

> I looked about for happiness, but could not find it. Then I thought, "O, if I had but such a person with me, I would surely be happy."
> I mused with myself, "How lovely is her look! How agreeable she talks!" I thought of Sappho's words:
>
>> "Blessed as th' immortal gods is he,
>> The youth that fondly sits by thee;

---

[12]Jeremy Taylor, "The Marriage Ring," or "The Mysteriousness and Duties of Marriage," *Master Sermons Through the Ages*, ed. William Alan Sadler, Jr. (New York: Harper & Row, 1963), 113. Originally found in *The Whole Works of the Right Reverend Jeremy Taylor*, vol. 5 (London: W. Clowes, 1828).

And hears and sees thee all the while
Softly speak and sweetly smile."

"Surely this is the very thing I want; and could attain it, I should then be no more solitary! For—

'Thou, from all darkness would exclude,
And from a desert banish solitude'"

…Let me, then, ask you a few questions. Were you ever convinced of sin? of your lost undone state?…If therefore, you are not happy now, is it not because you have not that intercourse with God which you then had? And are you seeking to supply the want of that intercourse by the enjoyment of a creature? You imagine that your connection with a woman will make amends for distance from God?[13]

If available written resources are any indication, in many places in America during the nineteenth century the wedding sermon was omitted in many marriage ceremonies. Textual resources are scarce. This seems odd in view of several facts. First, nineteenth-century forms of discourse of all types were popular, including gatherings for dramatic readings of well-known prose and poetry, public recitations (reminiscent of the Bible verse recitation contest in *Tom Sawyer*), and the Chatauqua circuit and political debates featuring notable orators. Sermon collections are replete with all types of occasional sermons such as those given at dedications, anniversaries, and national holidays. Funeral sermons, too, were a notable and ever-present occasional sermon genre.

However, an overview of the wedding service in some nineteenth-century books of worship indicates little evidence of the wedding sermon. It is possible that the lack of theologically trained personnel in many areas made it feasible to serve primarily as a witness to a service rather than to include an address or homily.

<hr>

[13]John Wesley, "A Thought About Marriage," in James H. Potts, *Living Thoughts of John Wesley* (New York: Hunt & Eaton, 1891), 400–401.

One wedding sermon that has been preserved was preached by C. F. W. Walther at his daughter's wedding. Walther is known as the founder of Missouri Synod Lutheranism in America. The marriage was that of first cousins, so familial phrasing figures heavily in the preaching. The sermon structure is based on a Mosaic blessing that Walther uses as his outline for the sermon. The language of the preaching is passionate, loving, sentimental, and biblical, and ends with an eschatological reminder:

> Yes, my children, I bespeak you this peace as my last blessing. If this rules in your heart, you, my dear son, will have strength to love your wife as Christ loved the church, to rule over her in love and to bear her weaknesses; and you, my daughter, will have strength not only to love your husband as your lord but also to honor and to fear him and to be obedient to him in all things. And your marriage will be happily, a blessed marriage…lovely picture of Christ's marriage to the church, His eternal bride. And when finally your hour comes, you will fall asleep in peace, to awake there in the mansions of eternal peace.[14]

Conclusion

A historical reading of wedding sermons over the centuries offers contemporary ministers rich resources for the development of their own wedding preaching. This occurs in a number of ways. First, the reader will note that there is a predictable set of topics that have generally remained the same over the millennia. These topics were molded into sermons through a prismatic combination of denominational theology, scriptural usage, and the social demands and realities of the given context.

These topics continue to provide sustenance to the sermon writer: There are such common emphases as the duties

---

[14]C. F. W. Walther, "My Threefold Fatherly Blessing Upon You," in Aug. R. Suelflow, ed., *Selected Writings of C. F. W. Walther: Selected Sermons,* trans. Henry J. Eggold (St. Louis: Concordia, 1981), 187.

and obligations of married life, marriage as vocation (or estate in life), God's blessings, the communal ramifications of married life, exhortations about preserving the married state, and the relating of the married relationship to eschatological concerns.

There are, however, some differences between twentieth-century proclamation and early wedding sermons that the contemporary preacher must take into account. First, general views of human sexuality have shifted in the twentieth century to the extent that sexuality is viewed as healthy, a godly gift, and an intrinsic part of a good marriage for both male and female partners. In conjunction with this, the role of women has changed significantly to the extent that the topics of wifely obedience, childbearing, and submission to the husband either are canceled out or take on different interpretations.

Second, community structures have changed substantially from older forms, and it is important for today's preacher to decide just how that is presented in the sermon: Divorce, remarriage, relatives living at a distance, and often anonymous, larger congregations all have a bearing on this. Facile expectations of community support in a wedding sermon today are sentimental and inappropriate if support structures don't justify them.

Third, the use of biblical texts has also changed. Older forms of textual interpretation make contemporary use of such hermeneutical tactics as allegory awkward if not incomprehensible to modern ears, as well as doing violence to the texts themselves. Furthermore, today's wedding preachers now find a freedom available to them in preaching on almost any applicable biblical text rather than the older prescribed canon of texts, such as the Song of Songs, the wedding at Cana, or Ruth and Naomi's words (most of which were preached without actual reference to who was saying what).

Finally, what periodically peeks through the texts over the centuries is the preacher's sense of humor! Taylor's examples about not exciting the tempers of the other spouse and Luther's wholehearted admonition to the couple to delight in their marriage are reasons for contemporary preachers to ponder the judicious use of humor in wedding preaching as not only useful but a realistic reflection of the humor, even hilarity, in married life.

While the wedding sermon is considered a "may" rubric in many faith perspectives, the question that it still continues to raise for the preacher on the brink of the twenty-first century is: In a radically pluralistic setting today, how do I proclaim a theology of marriage that is incarnationally, scripturally, and historically faithful to the call of the gospel to individuals and communities?

4

Choosing Texts for the Wedding Sermon

The three subjects of texts, topics, and context, as constitutive of a proclaimed theology of marriage, are inextricably linked together. Separate discussion of each subject provides an artificial distinction only for purposes of analysis. This and the next two chapters form an interrelated view of the wedding sermon, with biblical texts as the starting point.

If those attending weddings were asked which texts they associate with such a service, even the most biblically illiterate would probably list at least one of these four: one of the versions of creation from Genesis; John 2:1–12; 1 Corinthians 13; and Ruth 1:16, 17. The frequent use of these particular texts has made them almost as familiar to the faithful as to those who are unchurched.

Amusingly, these well-known texts actually say nothing about marriage. The Genesis account speaks of human relationships within the context of God's creativity; the text from John, while describing a wedding, has nothing directly to do with the couple or the wedding, nor does it have any pronouncements of Jesus on marriage! The issue concerns a good drink and the meaning of Jesus' power. The Corinthians text is addressed urgently, not sentimentally, to a community in severe conflict. And the Ruth text is a declaration of loyalty between a woman and her mother-in-law.

If the same people were asked *why* any of these texts are used at weddings, closer examination of the texts would make their responses more ambiguous and diverse.

The use of biblical texts as the basis for a wedding sermon raises a set of significant, basic questions. First, why do we use scriptural texts at all in a wedding sermon? Second, what functions do biblical texts serve? Third, what guidelines are available for choice and use of scriptures in the wedding homily? Finally, what connection do they have with specific topics related to marriage?

Another common feature of many wedding sermons is the use of *nonscriptural* texts from a variety of resources. Of all preaching genre, wedding sermons draw on materials outside of the Bible to the greatest extent. The same set of questions, however, applies to these materials as to biblical texts.

In each case, text choices are just as prone to abuse as to appropriate use. What are the problems associated with the aesthetics and theology of poor text choices? What can be done to avoid them?

Scriptural Wedding Texts: What's the Use?

Many wedding sermons are not actually proclamation on biblical texts, although texts may, in fact, be read at some point in the wedding service. So, why have a specifically scripturally-based sermon? The central answer is a historical one. The acts of human community, worship, relationship-building—such as marriage—find a comprehensive, continuous voice in the narratives and rules of biblical texts over the centuries. A Christian wedding is not an isolated event unrelated to the hermeneutical play of texts in many times and places. Texts, like both the couple and the assembly, have a history—often surprisingly well known at many levels to the listeners.

The second reason is that it is the proclaimer's responsibility to construct from these prior witnesses a theology of marriage vis-à-vis the text(s) that offers a means of envisioning the wedding's meaning for both the couple and the assembled community. Obviously, personal, denominational, and clerical views will determine if this is a central reason or even relevant at all to the wedding ceremony.

While the pastor acts as a witness to the event of the couple's marrying one another, preaching based on scripture at a wedding provides the threshold for an integrative and cohesive way of viewing the event for all present. At its core, responsible wedding proclamation is a fix on the *meaning* of the event, not just a witnessing of it, celebrating it, or glorifying its beauty and reality.

As David Buttrick's recent assessment of proclamation notes:

> The—primary—task of ministry is not caring, for all kinds of people can offer devoted care; nor is it counseling, for there are able professionals who counsel; nor is it church management, for managers abound. No, the primary task of ministry is *meaning*. If we are ministers of meaning, then we had better learn to think theologically.[1]

Preaching a wedding sermon in conjunction with a biblical text presents to the proclaimer the question, What are we to make of this? The meaning-making and the marry-making of a wedding sermon have the witness and assistance of biblical texts to answer the question.

The Function of Texts

Before addressing the guidelines for text choices, the matter of meaning must begin with the *functions* texts can serve. It

---

[1]David Buttrick: *A Captive Voice: The Liberation of Preaching* (Louisville: Westminster/ John Knox Press, 1994), 110.

is an obvious hermeneutical fact, although sometimes a tragic one, that texts can serve almost any function, ranging from the oppressive to the ludicrous. Several checks and balances can assist in determining the appropriate functions of a text and pastoral construal of meaning for a given wedding.

One of the primary determinants is how the minister's denomination figures in the use of scriptural wedding texts. Are there any key statements from the Hebrew Scriptures, the Apocryphal books, or the New Testament related to marriage that tend to receive emphasis as core theological doctrine for a denomination in either a formal or popular sense?

Texts serve a number of functions denominationally; they can underscore denominational ideas of marriage, be highly selective in scope, and exclude other extrascriptural materials as improper, irrelevant, or in poor taste. Text selection may be confined to some parts of the Bible. For example, the inter-testamental books of the Apocrypha are rarely heard outside of Roman Catholic or Episcopal settings. Texts may serve as prompts or function as introductions to denominational views of the duties, functions, and obligations of the married.

Texts also have a denominational history, with earlier wedding proclamation emphasizing some themes that have now dropped out of usage to some extent. The eschatological theme, often based on texts from the book of Revelation, is an example of this. On the other hand, other texts persist over time; readings from the book of Tobit are still used today and have a long history associated with wedding preaching.

A further refinement of the denominational use of texts has to do with the use of various translations of scripture. Are these denominationally approved or available? Regardless of the text choice, some translations can result in language that is either appropriate and inclusive or archaic, sexist, and slanted. If lectors unknown to the presiding minister are part of the wedding liturgy, it is advisable to check with them well before the ceremony because some readers bring their own translations of scripture.

The preacher must begin with a text's sermonic function by noting the many possibilities that the genre of wedding sermons offer. The "genre direction" of a wedding sermon is specified and established by focusing on sermonic intentionality. What does the preacher hope to accomplish with the listeners in the wedding homily? One particular thing? several? Potentially, the sermon can do one or several of the following: instruct, enlighten, challenge, comfort, encourage, recall, hope, exhort, praise, warn, rejoice, and promise. This is more than a matter of pastoral tone or texts, but instead ranges over the entire theology of marriage developed in the sermon. However, rather than try to accomplish all of these legitimate goals and hopes, the proclaimer should settle on one or two at the most.

Particular texts may reflect the most well known generic Christian views related to marriage, such as the 1 Corinthians 13 text on love. Text choices, emerging from a couple's decision, can espouse a shared commitment, a comprehensive way of understanding their relationship, or an "agenda" to live out during the marriage. Texts may be as specific as the focus on the couple or as inclusive as a word to the entire Christian community or a combination of both.

Some biblical passages are chosen repeatedly in some faith perspectives because they exemplify a code of expectations and obligations for the couple. In a more comprehensive sense, such texts, along with other well-known texts, form the basic denominational metaphors that buttress views of marriage. Paul's metaphor for marriage of the relationship between Christ and the church is an example of a root metaphor used in Roman Catholic wedding homilies as a means of supporting a sacramental view of marriage.

Texts also inevitably form part of the narrative of the wedding service. What kind of stories do they tell, and are they in keeping with the other parts of the service? Texts can intentionally act as a counterpoint to some of the typical themes of the service. For example, while the day is festive, the text may provide a somber commentary on the responsibilities and struggles that will come with a new relationship; while promises are made on the wedding day, a counter may be found in texts related to the inevitable changes that make life a set of precipices and choices. Employing this type of liturgical-homiletical dialectic is a way of framing texts and forming sermon structure simultaneously.

Guidelines for Text Choices

In seeking to articulate the meaning of a particular wedding, the preacher must address a set of guidelines. While texts have multiple functions, what are some of the kaleidoscopic realities further imposed by denominational choices, pastoral assessment, and the marrying couple? The following checklist will serve wedding sermon preparation well in assessing both required and variable elements related to biblical text choices:

1. Does the denomination suggest, emphasize, or even require certain texts? Are lists of such texts available in books of worship, occasional service books, or printed orders of service? Is the pastor free to choose any texts or to omit them?

2. What roles do each of these scriptural collections play in text choice: Hebrew Scripture, the Apocryphal books, the New Testament? Are some privileged over others for use?

3. In liturgical traditions, should or do the texts have any consonance with the liturgical season at hand? (In some instances churches do not have weddings during particular seasons, such as Lent.) Are wedding sermons denominationally focused through reference to the church season?

4. Who chooses the texts? the pastor? the couple? both? As a result of the choices, who and what are reflected therein? Are there any texts on which the minister chooses not to preach?

5. Are those who choose the texts clear about their reasons for placement and functioning in the service?

6. How do the text choices affect the genre direction of the sermon? What do they intend to do?

7. How does choice of Bible translation affect the perceived meanings of the texts?

8. How will text choice potentially affect listeners: couple, congregational members, visitors, churched, unchurched, generationally, and in terms of gender?

9. Who reads the texts? how? why?[2]

10. What theology of marriage is the proclaimer at tempting to establish by a given set of text choices?

The play of texts, service, and participants seems to offer the preacher an almost endless set of choices. However, the choices may be more bounded than one might think at first glance.

Extrabiblical Texts

The second major reality that crops up frequently in wedding sermons is the broad array of nonscriptural texts.[3] This can happen for several reasons. Nonscriptural texts are used and valued historically, since wedding discourse has such a mixed church/state history. In other words, what exactly constitutes a text and topics for wedding discourse remains open for debate, since the ecclesial and the cultural are so consistently blurred over time and since marriage is a topic held in common in all phases of human community. The frequent quotations, both positive and negative, from Sappho are an excellent example of this "war of the texts."

---

[2]For an excellent discussion of wedding texts see Graziano Marcheschi with Nancy Seitz Marcheschi, *Scripture at Weddings: Choosing and Proclaiming the Word of God* (Chicago: Liturgy Training Publications, 1992). This text is specifically geared for a Roman Catholic audience, but for that very reason it offers Protestant readers a useful means of comparison regarding theologies of marriage, topic choice, and textual emphases.

[3]See appendix A. I am indebted to Pastor David von Schlichten for his contributions to this list.

Often the couple may have specific requests for the use of such texts, including everything from the *Rubáiyát* of Omar Khayyám to prose pieces of different sorts. These texts, like a significant piece of music, may have played some role in the couple's relationship. Sometimes couples will choose such texts because they have heard them read at friends' weddings. It is possible that such a text may even be composed by one of them or by a friend or relative.

A third possibility is that the pastor may have found a text or texts that have worked in wedding sermons and cherishes this particular nonscriptural or anecdotal approach.

There are many, many possibilities for nonscriptural texts in the wedding sermon: a story, mnemonic device (object lesson even), poem, joke, riddle, fairy tale, children's story, newspaper or journal article, a form of autobiography or biography, letter or excerpts from one, recipe, road map, floor plan, scripture from faith traditions other than the one in which the service is being held, verses of songs and/or hymns, something of the couple's own composition, prayers, blessings, and proverbial sayings. Some of these verbal pieces may even be interspersed with music. The use of audiovisual resources as part of the overall sermon text is also a possibility.

Perhaps the most difficult question to answer for such texts is the functional one. Why use these texts when scriptural texts and their exposition are available? What do they add to the sermon? Are they a distraction? The typical answer is again one of meaning and is often readily answered by the couple suggesting the extrabiblical text: This text best sums up our relationship or what we intend with the marriage. The response may be even more general: "We like this and want it in the service."

There are several guidelines to consider in the sometimes treacherous waters of nonscriptural text usage in wedding proclamation. The proclaimer and couple need to answer the following questions:

1. What is the rationale for using it?

2. What is the source of the piece? Beyond the personal answers, there are also pragmatic issues. Do copyright laws apply? How will the preacher distinguish it verbally from other parts of the sermon as a quote?

3. How long is the selection? What genre is it?

4. Is anyone's privacy violated by the use of a particular nonscriptural text?

5. What is the theology in the piece, and does it conflict with the religious context and text of the sermon and setting? Does the piece include metaphors that are or are not reflective of, or maybe even contradictory to, the Christian faith?

6. Is the piece offensive at any level? aesthetically? morally? scripturally? sexually? theologically?

7. To whom is the piece addressed: God, the couple, the families, the worshipers, everyone?

8. What does its use contribute to the sermon?

Abuses of Texts

The power of choosing, interpreting, and proclaiming texts is enormous. What abuses of scriptural and nonscriptural texts should the preacher avoid? Contrary to the somewhat jaundiced opinion that "Nobody hears anything at a wedding," the opportunity to speak and speak textually makes an enormous impact on listeners. It is also an impact over which we have little control and few means of discerning as proclaimers.

First, scriptural text choice and interpretation may be perverted by radical eisegesis. As part of the hermeneutical expression of the preacher, the issue of a pastor's personal feelings does come into play, however implicitly. It is possible to knowingly create interpretations that violate in some way all the participants at a wedding.

The opening illustration in this volume from Amlin Gray's play *Kingdom Come* features a pastor who uses a damning text from the book of Hosea at a marriage to homiletically berate the couple and their friends for emigrating to America! While this is an extreme and open instance of pastoral dismay concerning a wedding, it is essential nevertheless to monitor one's own sense and estimation of the couple. Inevitably pastoral concerns will color the tone of the homily. A recent remark from a pastor waiting for a couple half an hour late for their own wedding was: "The later they are, the shorter this will be!"

However, it is not the texts themselves so much as the pastor's powers of hermeneutical creativity that are at stake. Several major problems can express themselves in sermons in this regard. It can mean choosing texts that demean the participants at some level—such as reinforcing outmoded views of women or the roles of the individuals in married life.

Texts can wrench marriage away from a frankly incarnational faith approach. Weddings are about bodies and what they do and do not do with one another. It is pastorally wrong to preach a view of marriage that sentimentalizes, idealizes, overlooks, or avoids the radical social reality of individuals and their communities. Love *does* mean being able to say that one *is* sorry.

Preachers may also form sermons from both scriptural or extrabiblical texts that are trite and "catchy." One example from bad-wedding-sermon lore was a pastor's repeated use of the children's game of Rock, Scissors, Paper. Not only was the device clever mnemonically, but it eventually became known as the parish's main source of triteness at weddings, given the repetitive use to which the pastor put it. The basic sin of such an approach is the way it trivializes the events at hand. It also lends subtle credence to the unfortunate analogy that marriage is a "game."

A somewhat related sermonic problem is the fashioning of sermons that are strictly decorative in nature. No attempt is made to lend a vision, instruct, affirm, or challenge those marrying. Sermon material is held radically separate from anything except a purely aesthetic or romantic view of marriage.

Texts' proclamation may also simply miss the couple who are marrying. If the preacher has spent little or no time with them, the risk of choosing inappropriate texts and topics is a major possibility. If something special distinguishes this couple to the community, or if the circumstances of the wedding itself are noteworthy, it is crucial that the pastor's homiletical choices show cognizance of that.

Another problem associated with textual preaching at weddings is that the texts can simply emerge as text commentary but result in no creative conclusions of any type of a theology of marriage. In other words, the texts remain at the thinly veiled exegetical level with no hermeneutical distances covered regarding custom, the couple, and the assembly or denomination. This makes of preaching something incantational or mantralike in form—a sentimental commentary on a text with nothing extrapolated or fashioned from it that speaks meaningfully to the community of faith.

The latitude for abuse with nonscriptural texts is also great. Such instances include the following: The chosen selection may be completely unfamiliar and therefore distracting to the hearers; its meaning may be discernible only to the couple. It can be so vivid or unusual that it disrupts the overall flow of the sermon. Occasionally, long pieces may be preferred by the couple. Such texts may outweigh in length and emphasis the specified biblical texts for the day or will suffer problems related to content and meaning through pastoral editing. Some texts are simply in poor taste.

While text choices are possible and numerous, the basic question the pastor and couple must ask is, Is this text consonant with the meanings intended in the overall wedding service and proclamation?

Conclusion

Texts used in wedding ceremonies over the centuries may be a combination of scriptural and extrabiblical passages. First, the use of biblical texts provides topics that fix a sermon within a particular denominational and personal context. Although choice of scriptures varies, it does not do so widely from denomination to denomination. Like ecumenical Sunday lectionary preaching, there are many commonalities among wedding text choices.

The use of extrabiblical texts offers many resources to the preacher, but also presents significant theological, aesthetic, and social issues and pressures. In the case of both scriptural and nonscriptural texts, the preacher must exercise care with the way in which these are chosen separately and how they might sound in combination with one another. The minister will need to carefully consider denominational, personal, and parish guidelines as to how and by whom wedding sermon materials are chosen.

5

Choosing Topics for the Wedding Sermon

The possible topics for a wedding sermon are virtually endless. The topical sources of Christian wedding proclamation may start with scripture, be placed in conjunction with it, use nonscriptural texts, or combine these possibilities into some type of theology of marriage. Above all else, the living text of the marrying couple provides the connective tissue for all other discourse decisions and subjects. This chapter will look at some of the common and uncommon topics derived from historical, biblical, and personal sources for use in the wedding sermon, as well some new configurations of traditional topics.

The search for sermon topics is ancient. Martin Luther noted with disgust how some pastors of his era approached the problem of finding preaching topics:

> Everything that they are to teach and preach is now available to them in clear and simple form in the many excellent books which are in reality what the old manuals claimed in their titles to be: "Sermons That Preach Themselves," "Sleep Soundly," "Prepared!" and "Treasury." However, they are not so upright and honest as to buy these books, or if they have them to examine

and read them. Such shameful gluttons and servants of their bellies would make better swineherds or dogkeepers than spiritual guides and pastors.[1]

Historically, topical preaching choice is listed in both sermons and theoretical manuals. Any era of preaching shows that the theological, legal, and social moods are highly determinative of the views of female and male in marriage and are mirrored in the sermons of the time. Older medieval pastoral and preaching manuals offered *exempla* for use in sermons. Something like a theological *Aesop's Fables*, the preacher could select those moralistic sections that fit his needs. Topical emphases over the past centuries have included explicit and lengthy instructions regarding the duties of the wife in marriage. The issue of household authority, based on Paul's concept of headship in the church and the created order, dominates admonitions to the male to act as head of the household.

Another subject is the role of children in the marriage: They can be considered a duty with regard to the marriage, a blessing, a means of maintaining the family name, and a sign of God's favor. Although this topic has continued into the end of the twentieth century, it has been modified. Divorce statistics, a drop in the birth rate, and other trends in personal and familial stewardship have changed or muted this element to some extent. These approaches still continue in a variety of ways today, although affected in some cases more by cultural and political perspectives than by any actual denominational stance.[2]

If any kind of generalization can be made at all about the topical shifts and text usage in the Christian wedding sermon over the centuries, it appears that the emphasis is now more focused on what couples bring to marriage (e.g., identity issues,

---

[1]Martin Luther, "Large Catechism," in *Book of Concord*, trans. and ed. Theodore G. Tappert (Philadelphia: Muhlenberg Press, 1959), 358.

[2]One example of a current organization that has focused on the roles of married life is Promise Keepers, founded by Bill McCartney. It is for men only and is specific about the obligations and duties of married life. For an overview of the Promise Keepers' precepts and views, see the article in *Christian Century*, March 6, 1996.

creativity), rather than emphasizing the expectations and obligations of church and society toward the couple. Some of this is due to changes in the intentionality of wedding preaching: The approach is focused more on encouragement than exhortation, based on long-standing traditional codes of marital behavior. Changes in theological and moral codes of prescribed behavior and the continually evolving changes in the relationships between women and men have influenced the sermon. Denominational views and requirements for marriage have also been blurred in many places through interfaith weddings, thereby affecting subject choices. Additionally, ministers are often faced with the prospect of preaching at weddings for couples who have little or no religious interest or affiliation; traditional religious mores have little value or meaning in such contexts (see Sermon #3 in chapter 8).

For the preacher, topical choice has become both more difficult and more interesting! However, selection of topics from biblical and extrabiblical sources must come primarily from the pastoral interpretation of the lives of the marrying couple. If this is obviated in any way, wedding proclamation will be formulaic and lack depth of meaning. Here, premarital counseling can open the door to pertinent homiletical creativity. One individual, reflecting on remarriage after the death of a spouse, enters a plea for the relational aspects of wedding sermon preparation between the pastor and couple:

> If I were sitting with the pastor whom I had asked to marry me and my fiancee, I would not, quite frankly, want to talk about topics for the wedding sermon. I would, out of the pastoral conversation about us (our hopes, intentions, understandings, griefs, etc.), want to give to my pastor the task of focusing on what should/ could be said in an appropriate sermonic way at the wedding. We would have talked already about hymns, scripture, prayers, etc., and that also would be some indication about us as a couple and about our intention to exchange vows in marriage. But in the end, the focus

of the sermon is the pastor's. And quite honestly, I would hesitate having someone preach at my wedding who had not been involved in pastoral conversation/relationship with us enough to be able to do this. If anything, I guess that this shows how important a pastoral relationship is for me, not only in preaching for marriages, but in any ritual connected with the faith that has both a personal and public dimension.[3]

Locating Scriptural Topics

There are several approaches to uncovering topics. First, the topics can readily reveal themselves through the texts chosen for the wedding. Here, the preacher runs a fine line between preaching on topics derived from the text and simply using the texts as a prompt for adjacent matters or for a sermon strictly topical and nontextual in nature. While there is nothing wrong with the latter approach, it again raises the question about the function—if any—that a text has in a wedding service.

The pastor's work in the study offers many other sources of topics. If the context strongly suggests a particular topic, a concordance is particularly useful. Translations of a particular word or thought can open the door to the appropriate sermon approach. Knowledge of Greek and Hebrew is helpful, but if the preacher is not trained in these, an interlinear translation and accompanying dictionary are invaluable. Knowing the context of a passage may also lend heightened meaning to a text. The fact that 1 Corinthians 13 was shared with a community in deep conflict stakes out the cost and contours of what it means to love in a radically realistic way—an appropriate homiletic goal on a wedding day.

One type of biblical passage that easily offers topics is that featuring a list: Philippians 4:8, "Finally beloved, whatever is true, whatever is honorable, whatever is just, whatever is pure,

---

[3]Anonymous.

whatever is pleasing, whatever is commendable, if there is any excellence and if there is anything worthy of praise, think about these things."

Another list, found in 1 Corinthians 13, features the well-known attributes of love and what it is not. Paul's listings of the fruits of the spirit make one or all of these topics worth the preaching: "The fruit of the Spirit is love, joy, peace, patience, kindness, generosity, faithfulness, gentleness, and self-control" (Gal. 5:22–23).

The core of scripturally suggested topics for wedding proclamation is well known, and some of these texts may come with a couple's strong recommendation for use. It is up to the preacher to think of preaching these in ways that avoid triteness and strike an honest tone throughout the homily.

Theological and Liturgical Topics

Topics set at one or more removes from primary scriptural texts offer rich resources. A significant and enduring list from the Reformation is still helpful for offering potential preaching topics. It comes from one of the Reformation era's chief lay theologians, Philip Melanchthon, teacher and rhetorician, trained in classical rhetoric.

While his list of topics is set within the highly polemical era in which he wrote, it continues to offer the contemporary preacher a superlative entree to the construction of the wedding sermon. It also shows the extent to which theologizing expands the perimeters of the biblical texts. The following list divides itself generally into topics having to do with theological and social realities.

In our churches, on the other hand, all sermons deal with topics like these:

Penitence, the fear of God, faith in Christ, the righteousness of faith, comfort for the conscience through faith, the exercise of faith, prayer and our assurance that it is efficacious and is heard, the cross, respect for

rulers and for all civil ordinances, the distinction between the kingdom of Christ (or the spiritual kingdom) and political affairs, marriage, the education and
instruction of children, chastity, and all the works of
love. From this description of the state of our churches
it is evident that we diligently maintain church discipline, pious ceremonies, and the good customs of the
church.[4]

How does one fashion such topics in accordance with a
denominational theology of marriage? Another topical
possibility that covers all relationship scenarios and denominational perspectives is that of identifying the major gatekeeping
liturgical emphases in a given faith community as a source of
sermon topics. This varies. A key element in many faith communities is baptism, sometimes characterized as a sacrament.
The act of baptism bears its own vast array of symbols, definitions, and meanings, some of which can be incorporated into
the wedding sermon. Topics it suggests are approaches to life,
marriage as a call to the gospel and vocation, the sharing of
community in particular ways, the source of spiritual renewal
for daily life and marriage, and a sacrament of continuity and
family.

The same may also be said for the Lord's supper (or variously, communion, the holy supper, eucharist, the mass, the
meal). As a preaching focus, this meal can act as a sign of involvement in community, reconciliation, global participation,
a sign of unity, a meal, *viaticum*—for the marriage journey, an
inclusionary metaphor reflective of a couple's commitments
to the marriage and service to others. This should not be a
preaching subject in a central fashion unless the service actually incorporates this action. From other perspectives, the function of God's word, particularly as it is found in the books of
the Bible, becomes significant. The devotional and spiritual

---

[4]Philip Melanchthon, "Article XIV. Of Human Traditions," *Apology of the Augsburg Confession,* in *Book of Concord: The Confessions of the Evangelical Lutheran Church,* trans. and ed. Theodore G. Tappert (Philadelphia: Muhlenberg Press, 1959), 221.

life of a couple, the unfolding of the marriage, may all be related to the centrality of God's word (however defined) in the marriage. The preacher may even wish to select a specific Bible verse or set of verses, apart from and/or as part of the sermon, to give to the couple as a charter for their marriage. Select phrases or sentences from the liturgy, whether biblical or otherwise, can also offer possibilities. Some of the available sources are the creeds, hymns, blessings, and prayers.

Preaching Honestly

A less-than-realistic note about marriage is a characteristic of many wedding sermons. A romantized, idealized vision of wedding proclamation is next to useless. The pastor should not, however, think honest expression about real and potential marriage issues will be thought of as simply speaking negatively.

Of historical note is such a collection of quasi-sermons from Harriet Beecher Stowe titled *Little Foxes.*[5] The sermons are a response to the text from the Song of Songs: "Catch us the foxes, the little foxes, that ruin the vineyards—for our vineyards are in blossom." (Song 2:15). The sermons include a number of bad habits, all those "little foxes," that can destroy human community and are couched first in the negative.

This type of preaching, while dated somewhat in terms of the exhortatory style, is in no way humanly dated—it is simply honest. Any preaching like this should not use negative topics in and of themselves, but in accordance with statements of affirmation concerning content, goals, and dreams in a marriage. In other words, is there a concluding and overall counter to any unsettling issues raised, a means of sounding the gospel's good news as well as the law?

One preacher's frank estimation of marriage included first a comment on the potential antitheses to reconciliation:

> Perhaps you don't think I should even speak of hostility on this occasion, for you are occupied with thoughts of love for each other and have not the slightest

---

[5]Harriet Beecher Stowe, *Little Foxes* (Boston: Ticknor and Fields, 1866).

intention of allowing anything to disturb the very close relationship into which you are entering. Yet the latent hostility is there, and if you are realistic, you will face it. Men are always complaining that they do not understand women—by which they mean that they do not approve of the way women's minds work, the attitudes they take toward life, and the methods they use to get what they want. Women, for their part, often resent men for a variety of reasons and do what they can to change them. In the close contact of married life this mutual antagonism may flare into a serious disagreement and often does. [6]

A student at Lutheran Theological Seminary at Gettysburg, married for a year, preached a wedding-oriented sermon within an engagement-encounter type weekend setting.[7] Rather than focusing on the usual corpus of topics, she chose the topic of enmity. The sermon opened with a published description of one couple's breakdown in communication. She then described the inarticulate anger she and her spouse had experienced toward one another on one issue over a period of time. The deep power struggles of the married life were focused through Romans 8:26. "Likewise the Spirit helps us in our weakness; for we do not know how to pray as we ought, but that very Spirit intercedes with sighs too deep for words."

The sermon posed the question, "Where to next, if we aren't able to pray or even speak to each other because of the pain?" It was not only heartfelt, but the reaction of the listeners, almost all of them married, was notable; everyone wished that they had heard that particular type of preaching before instead of after their own weddings.

The sermon could not be classified under exhortation but was the simple sharing of a deeply distressing episode in a marriage and profoundly affected all who heard it.

---

[6]Herbert Lindemann, "Preservation for Life's Paths," in *Wedding Addresses* (St. Louis: Concordia, 1955), 46–47.

[7]Used with permission of Tiffany Jeske Hall (Class of 1998, Lutheran Theological Seminary at Gettysburg).

Other contemporary topics may be the lack of communication, alcoholism and other addictions, communication failures, or the refusal to honor commitments. Obvious counters to these are at hand biblically from a number of perspectives.

Topics in a New Age

What new approaches to the topics of wedding preaching might one take? Actually, there are no new topics—simply new means of revisiting perennial realities that result from the interactions of couples. As we embark upon the twenty-first century, topics have emerged that are highly determinative of the health of a marital relationship. New insights in the social sciences and human relationships over the centuries have greatly expanded topical lists beyond Melanchthon's succinct note of "marriage" as a preaching topic.

As a result of pastoral marriage and family practices over the years, married interactions have been identified in a number of ways. One perspective on such dynamics that offers potential wedding sermon material is taken from a Pennsylvania counseling practice and is used in the marriage counseling course at Gettysburg Lutheran Theological Seminary at Gettysburg.[8] The marital relationship is discussed through the lenses of four major operative interactions in marriage: freedom, intimacy, power, and security. Each reality is invariably a part of a marriage relationship and can be enacted on a spectrum that builds toward a healthy or unhealthy relationship. Taken separately or as a group, these offer significant subjects for premarital counseling as well as for a wedding sermon.[9]

These interactions have several strengths as preaching topics. First, they are topics that are essentially neutral in content, malleable as far as their workings in relationships and the

---

[8]Dr. Norma Schweitzer Wood, instructor and dean of Lutheran Theological Seminary at Gettysburg, and Dr. Herbert W. Stroup, Jr., professor emeritus, Lutheran Theological Seminary at Gettysburg, developed this taxonomy from their counseling practice, Marriage and Family Counseling Associates, in York, Pennsylvania.

[9]See appendix B for a complete description of the taxonomy mentioned above.

preacher's sermonic definitions. Second, they are resonant with scripture and also adjacent to many other biblical and theological themes. Third, they are dynamics that can be heard by an entire community and are not restricted only to the marrying couple. Finally, these human responses are worked out from the perspective of the couple's interactions as well as each person's relationship to God, making of this model an incarnational form of proclamation at its best.

Another source of rich sermon topics is the identification of a particular activity or experience the couple shares that can provide a root metaphor for the hopes, issues, and future of the marriage. One proclaimer created a sermon using the metaphor of dancing/the dance for a couple involved in the theater. She drew on related illustrations of the Shaker tune "The Gift To Be Simple" ("Dance, dance, wherever you may be"), the dance of creation, the patterns and types of dancing, and the implications of partnership for the venture.

Another minister used the couple's involvement in Habitat for Humanity to speak of the habitats provided by marriage. Illustrations of nurturance, support, community, and safe haven and shelter were preached.

Metaphors can come from such diverse arenas as hobbies, sports, travels, and community and political involvements. They can not only yield sermonic topics and structure but also function to draw in the entire community around a common point of recognition and participation.

Conclusion

The creation of a wedding sermon depends on the interplay of several factors: the preacher's self-understanding and intentionality regarding a theology of marriage presented in the sermon; the pastoral time spent with the marrying couple; a clear understanding of the lives and circumstances of a couple, and finally, the selection of topics, which binds all of these realities together.

In order to avoid triteness, misunderstanding, and irrelevancy, the proclaimer must also be aware of topical resources and options other than the strictly biblical. These include attention to the dynamics of marriage, liturgical emphases in a denomination's faith life, resources from the fields of psychology and counseling, and shared metaphors.

6

A Theology of Marriage in Context

Two foundational questions are addressed in this chapter: First, what is a theology of marriage? Second, how can the life setting of the couple, together with suitable texts and topics, best exemplify a given theology of marriage? When preparing a wedding sermon, the preacher must find the appropriate blend of *context* (of the couple), *topic(s),* and *text(s)* that will result in a more intentional approach to a proclaimed theology of marriage. There are, however, basic questions to answer prior to sermon construction, and the first concerns a theology of marriage. Every wedding sermon represents a particular theology of marriage, however implicit or explicit; each is an amalgam of ideas, beliefs, feelings, and texts that are composed from several sources.

No attempt is made here to identify, critique, support, or emphasize a specific denominational theology of marriage; the task is too complicated and time-consuming and is actually a matter more for the historical theologian. However, it is, in fact, urgent that the preacher know clearly which elements constitute such a theology in a particular denomination in order to proclaim adequately and meaningfully.

It is a simple question: What is my denomination's theology of marriage? Most obviously, the denominational faith perspective represented by the clergy is the publicly acknowledged central voice in most wedding sermons. However, pastors will need to identify several resources in order to make sure they are clear about the answers to this question. A Roman Catholic wedding homily espousing a sacramental view of marriage, for example, will be quite different in theology from that of a nonsacramental approach preached by a Presbyterian officiant. Or, on the other hand, if marriage is understood basically as a social contract by members of a denomination, at what point does a church's perspective identify it as a matter of faith concern?

Second, the preacher's personal theology comes into play. This may or may not be at odds with the denominational theology professionally represented, but it does bear examination. It is at this juncture that both theology and ethos meet. What are the preacher's own experiences with love, marriage, sexuality, and relationships? What role do these play in the formation of a wedding sermon and in conversations with the marrying couple?

Does the preacher actually model or represent the married choice of life? Or are other realities operative—such as the preacher's being single vocationally (by choice or by circumstance), widowed, or divorced? And are the preacher's vocational choices echoed in the preaching in any way? If the congregation at the wedding is in any way acquainted with the officiant, one's station in life and the preacher's feelings and actions may or may not create dissonance in the experience of the listeners.

One potential nonverbal issue in proclamation at the wedding service is the gender of the pastor. If cultural and religious mores have traditionally regarded women as passive, without voice publicly, female pastoral leadership at a wedding may significantly affect the hearing of the homily. By the same token, the uniqueness of the wedding day may also include the uniqueness of participants of female leadership. Research is yet unavailable as to the implications of the officiant's marital status or gender for this particular worship setting, although the ethos of the presiding minister is a given reality that will speak homiletically in verbal and nonverbal ways.

All of the personal components a minister brings to sermon preparation involve her or his ethical stance concerning text choice. Text choice may be generally compatible with those suggested by the minister's denomination. But what happens if the minister's text choice is outside of the "approved list," or if the interpretation given to a text is radically different from accustomed usage intended by the church, the couple, or the denomination?

Obviously, the relationship between the pastor and marrying couple should involve discussions about the pastor's text guidelines for wedding sermons. The wedding pulpit is no place for homiletical surprises. It is one thing to give a couple a denominational scriptural list and ask them to choose a preaching text and quite another thing to use the same text homiletically in a way that does violence to the setting. As with choice of music for weddings, pastors must be clear initially about those texts they either will not read or preach on and/or the interpretations they plan to give texts that they do—at least in a general fashion. Wedding proclamation must find the narrow path between the mix of denominational and personal theologies. A wide divergence between the two indicates that there are vocational issues that extend far beyond wedding proclamation.

Next, what role, if any, has the homily or sermon had in the worship life of the parish? Has the congregation been accustomed to hearing wedding sermons? Have they heard the same one repeated at all weddings? Do they hear a denominational faith perspective? a mixture of faith and cultural views of the married life? If preached, has the sermon been based on scripture? Has it relied on its theology from extrabiblical sources, including other texts, traditions, history, and anecdotes of different sorts?

Fourth, how does the denomination understand marriage from a scriptural basis? Are there any key statements from the Hebrew Scriptures, the Apocryphal books, or the New

Testament that tend to be emphasized as core theological doctrine for a denomination either in a formal or popular sense?

Texts serve a number of functions denominationally; they can underscore denominational ideas of marriage, and they can be highly selective in scope and exclude other discourse as improper, irrelevant, or in poor taste. Text selection may be confined to some parts of the Bible. For example, the intertestamental books of the Apocrypha are rarely heard outside of Roman Catholic settings. Texts may serve as prompts or function as an introduction to the denominational views of the duties, functions, and obligations of marriage.

Texts also have a denominational history, with earlier wedding proclamation emphasizing some themes that have now dropped out of usage to some extent. The eschatological theme, often based on texts from the book of Revelation, is an example of this. On the other hand, others persist over time; readings from the book of Tobit are still used today and have a long history associated with wedding preaching.[1]

A further refinement of this question involves the use of different translations of scripture. Are these denominationally approved or available? Regardless of the text choice, such translations can result in language that is either appropriate and inclusive or archaic, sexist, and slanted.

Text choice is also a decision that one's pastoral theology of marriage leaves open. Does the pastor choose the text(s)? Are their denominational choices offered? What role does the couple have in this? What if they wish to choose texts that contradict the denomination's stance on marriage? For the pastor, what defines the boundaries of text choice?

Fifth, ministers will know the key historical documents of their church that speak to marriage. They will be aware of any current denominational issues and discussions and church

---

[1]See E. Schillebeeckx, O. P., *Marriage: Human Reality and Saving Mystery* (New York: Sheed and Ward, 1965), 277. The author notes that a reading from the book of Tobit was in place in eleventh- and twelfth-century marriage liturgies.

statements (the terminology varies) in the area of sexuality, family life, or marriage that may affect their listeners' lives. Does the denomination look to any particular theologian or group of theologians who have discussed marriage from their vantage point? The writings of those in pastoral theology, in particular, may be useful to the proclaimer.

Sixth, if clergy are new to an area, are there any regional or local religious perspectives that have deeply colored the theology of marriage in the parish? Whether the preacher agrees or disagrees with such things, it is important to be aware of what they are. This is not necessarily the same thing as overt customs, actions, or symbols used in the ceremony, but it relates to the type of discourse the preacher uses in framing marriage and faith views and values out of the traditions and history of the people in a particular place.

The Pastoral Relationship to the Couple

Most importantly, what role does the couple play in constructing a theology of marriage for a homily? It is this author's contention that the more specific and durable the pastoral relationship with a couple, the more in-depth will be the preaching and pastoral care. This is undoubtedly the catalyst for binding all the other elements of sermon construction together, since the couple's particular relationship will highlight specific elements of a theology of marriage.

Denominational views of the pastoral office, however, affect the extent to which this can be true for a minister's proclamation. In other words, a rhetorical fix on this question would ask, What role does denominationally prescribed pastoral ethos play in the wedding sermon? Approaches differ. The minister's central function might be as witness to the marriage, without a specifically personal voice.

It could be pastoral proclamation on prescribed texts of the tradition with a subtle pastoral voice. Another view of the officiant's function is the active inclusion of the couple in creating the homily. Occasionally, parish rules place this issue beyond the control of the minister. Clearly the denomination's view of the pastoral office in general will determine how meaning is construed in wedding proclamation.

It is up to the pastoral discernment of the preacher to elicit appropriate personal information from the couple that will guide topic and text choices and receive the most significant hearing from them and their community. Depending on how well the pastor knows the couple, participants may share in-depth concerns, realities, and dynamics that assist the proclaimer's sermon development. Others sometimes simply leave it to the minister to reflect homiletically on what their relationship is saying, and little self-disclosure is part of the pastoral/parishioner relationship.

While it is an idealistic hope to expect that the mosaic of time, minister, and couples will always result in a shared contribution to the homily, an established pastoral relationship with the couple can provide the key to a valuable nexus of conversation, counseling, and relationship-building focus for preparing the wedding sermon.

A pastor will be preaching to a group composed of the following: persons who are committed members of a particular faith community, persons who have only a minimal knowledge of Christianity, and persons who are religiously disinterested. Depending on the composition of the group, the proclaimer will have a number of corresponding homiletical decisions to make.

Frequently, couples may wish to bring one element to the sermon that the minister will take into consideration—interest in text choices. Ministers will want to structure how they discuss text possibilities with couples. Foremost, the hope for such an exchange will provide useful insight for the wedding homily and also enable the preacher to understand the couple's own theology of marriage.

The ministers can provide a list of suggested texts and ask the couple to read the passages prior to the next conversation.

Or the minister may want to give the couple a list of questions to ask of chosen texts: Why a given text? How does this text speak to our relationship and our hopes for the future? How does any text speak of God's blessing and activities in the marriage? What will these texts say about us to the assembly? Is there anything in a text that characterizes our relationship that we hope the preacher will note in the sermon?

Profiles of Couples

The plurality of marital circumstances is apparent in today's world and is inevitably reflected in the sermon. What are some of these life settings? The following list is certainly not exhaustive but is indicative of such circumstances: those marrying for the first time; remarriage after a divorce—with or without children involved; remarriage after the death of a spouse; interracial marriage; interfaith marriage; marriage where physical capabilities are an issue.

There are obviously many other types of marriage unions, but these are the most typical. Each of these life settings has realities and issues in common with the rest. Yet each is unique and suggests a specific cluster of possible preaching topics. Some couples may even represent a number of characteristics from two or more of the groups listed.

In constructing a wedding sermon, topic choice in response to couples' lives together needs to be rethought and broadened to a large extent. Couples marrying today often present life situations that appear to challenge or contradict biblical views of what constitutes healthy relationships. In the face of that, much of what is preached is trite and sometimes simply unrealistic—more of the hoped-for than an honest estimate of the inevitable and the real. Sometimes biblical perceptions of human community are freighted into contemporary preaching with no effort at a second hermeneutical look and, therefore, with disastrous effects.

It is possible that the preacher may wish to avoid truthful appraisals of the married life for painful personal reasons or is attempting to respond to the festivities of the day with sincere expressions of hope for the future at the expense of realism. However, the call to honesty on this day is an obvious gospel claim on the preacher, and pressures to preach otherwise must be resisted. As one seasoned veteran of the pulpit observed wryly, "It's a pity we don't hear some resounding sermons on the text, 'Fight the good fight!'"

The following profiles of typical couples seeking marriage relate only to topic possibilities. This is only artificially so, because the combination of texts, topics, and couples is actually almost endless. It is important to note the primary biblical texts suggested from each faith perspective out of which and to which the marriage is preached. These or other texts can be used in conjunction with the following list of possible topics.

The topics listed are suggestive but hardly exhaustive of sermonic possibilities.

First Marriage

For those marrying for the first time, newness defines this context. Several things are potentially typical of couples in this scenario. First, they are embarking on a new adventure. New relationships of all types will emerge, as well as new experiences and tensions; what these mean to pastor, couple, and the congregation regarding new relatives, new feelings, new decisions must be taken into account. This sense of newness is also combined with joy, celebration, and relief in response to the fact that the tensions and ambiguities of engagement will now have a new and recognizable public context—a marriage.

Another adjacent and reassuring topic, the continuity of the past, may indeed be a suitable topic for a first wedding, certainly a typical topic from ancient sources. However, one way continuity finds expression today resides in the fact that numerous couples have lived together before marriage. According to statistics, this may be the cultural substitute for lack of a betrothal ritual.[2] The pastor runs the risk of appearing

---

[2]John Shelby Spong, "Betrothal: An Idea Whose Time Has Come," in *Living in Sin? A Bishop Rethinks Human Sexuality* (San Francisco: HarperSanFrancisco, 1988).

naive in proclamation about the future prospects of shared daily life if this has been an ongoing reality in the past!

Another context matter is a maturity factor. Age will determine, at least in part, the gifts, skills, and education that both parties bring to the marriage and therefore the types of available wedding sermon topics.

The minister may also proclaim the value and reality of Christian marriage as vocation, sharing the images and obligations of living out marriage in cruciform shape. What does it mean to work within a marriage process where perceptions, feelings, thoughts, and actions are called to conform to the presence of the godly in the relationship?

The fear/reassurance dyad is another potential topic. However unspoken, the couple and the community, perhaps the pastor, may have reservations, even fears for the couple. Will this marriage work? Are these people equipped sufficiently to face this new relationship? Will this marriage, with the world's usual problems and barriers, end in divorce? What are the sources of our confidence and assurance in supporting this couple? What does the agape of God's love mean as the center of the crucible of human loving in a relationship—and that relationship in its community context?

Remarriage after Divorce

Entering the homiletical world of the divorced and then remarrying is problematic. This is obviously heightened by the degree to which the denomination censures divorce, supports the divorced, and works with those seeking to remarry—regardless of the details involved in any particular situation. The preacher is already confronted in such situations with the problem of how much to say or refrain from saying in this type of setting. Additionally, the presence of children from former marriages and their possible inclusion in the wedding service make it important to include some topics in a special way. Some of these can include belonging, conflicted loyalties, reconciliation, new beginnings, and the meaning of family.

One sermon approach is the use of God's promises as the prior category to all the promise-making and promise-keeping that individuals do, and do not do, with one another. The obvious reality at weddings of the remarrying divorced is that previous vows have been shattered. Reassurance of God's promises, forgiveness, and support are essential in this type of homily.

A related topic, that of grace and forgiveness, is proclaimed both theologically and interpersonally. That love can live again after the destruction of divorce is evidence of grace; that God forgives, redeems, and rebuilds is grace at work. That a couple may trust again and learn forgiveness between themselves and former spouses is a sign of grace interpersonally.

It may seem out of place to some to speak of forgiveness in such a blunt way within the context of a day that is not intended to be penitential in tone. However, it is quite possible that the wedding proclamation in this context offers a couple and their community a way to acknowledge the past and receive assurance of forgiveness in order to get on with the future. It is also the time to remind couples that, realistically, this new marriage will continually struggle with its own range of potential "divorcements."

Another subject central to marriage is that of God's faithfulness. God's initiative is that which births faith and confidence in the listeners whose hopes may be, at best, fragile and uncertain. Faithfulness can be related to the promise-making and -keeping of God and God's presence and love in all circumstances.

Remarriage after a Spouse's Death

Remarriage by those who have lost a spouse sets the tone, acknowledged or not, for several specific topics. The first is the reality of the past. The role of memory, remembrance, and the past must be pastorally present in such wedding proclamation.

In conjunction with the couple, the preacher may want to find ways to address the personality of the deceased spouse in a way that acknowledges the importance and effects of the last marriage into the present. The presence of young or adult children from a former marriage will certainly make this a reality.

One practice that taps a great array of meaning is the creedal affirmation and proclamation of the communion of saints. It deals not only with personalities but also with the working of God's love and providence through time, relationships, and all circumstances. In a related fashion, the topic of mystery, or God's providence, may be a helpful way to refocus the pain of loss, the ambiguity and joy of new relationships, and faith efforts to understand God's presence in changing events.

Another topic has to do with promises, though not only with the promises being made the couple on that day. It is essential to identify God's promises of life and renewal in this new marriage despite the context of grief (possibly even guilt) that can, on many levels, still persist and affect the new marriage. It is unrealistic to expect that a deceased spouse will not continue to have an impact on a new marriage, and a preacher should thoughtfully acknowledge the best parts of what was in terms of what can be.

Another fitting approach is confidence and reassurance for the future. The loss of a spouse to a terminal disease, and the often long, painful dying process accompanying it, scores the memories of many who remarry. This raises questions about the meanings of health, healing, and cure. It also raises fears that another relationship may go the same route. Since those remarrying under such circumstances are usually older, this topic holds much interest in view of another pending loss. Preaching in this setting not only acknowledges the past but offers reassurance and support for the future against the backdrop of what will inevitably be revisited in some form again.

The topic of God's creation of wholeness in the face of these ever-present human realities may be appropriate in some settings. If the dissolution of a marriage was marked by a sudden death, again the refashioning and reconstituting of life in

Christ, as evidenced in the new marriage, is another perspective. Certainly the amount of time that has elapsed between the loss and the remarriage will in part determine the pastor and couple's decision about the homiletical tone for the marriage.

Interracial or Intercultural Marriage

One type of marriage ceremony certain to elicit comment and concern in a supposedly pluralistic culture is an interracial marriage. The preacher's choice of topics should reflect honestly and clearly the basic reality of such a marriage—two individuals who love one another. From there, the pastoral conversations can determine how much the presence and union of two different cultures "matters" and the degree to which this must be reflected in the sermon.

The proclaimer must give a very attentive ear to the context of the couple's story of love, engagement, and proposed marriage. Exploration of significant cultural metaphors, symbols, and faith responses with the couple is a way of approaching the topics chosen for the homily.

Interfaith Marriage

An interfaith marriage definitely involves two specific factors that affect any message delivered at the ceremony: the possible presence of an officiant from another faith perspective and discussion with all concerned regarding the shared topics that can be addressed without division or rancor to all present at the wedding ceremony.[3]

The specific question for the proclaimer's sermon preparation is, What pool of topics are held in common by the Christian tradition and tradition X? It is here that the preacher will meet the religious and cultural boundaries of faith and community in some interesting ways. Again, it is the marrying couple who must have a significant voice in describing their

---

[3]See *How To Be A Perfect Stranger: A Guide to Etiquette in Other People's Religious Ceremonies,* ed. Jewish Lights Publishing Staff (Woodstock, Vt.: Jewish Lights Publishing, 1995).

faith perspectives to the preacher so that this is reflected fairly in the message.

Specific sacramental, creedal, theological, and faith community affirmations may necessarily be muted or secondary considerations in such settings. On the other hand, dynamics of virtue, morality, ethics, and values of the global community can receive more prominence.

Other Life Circumstances

Finally, one area that has received little attention but is enacted in many relationships is the wedding ceremony that features a couple, one or both partners of whom are physically challenged. This could be because of disease, chronic illness, birth defects, injury, or the effects of aging. None of these circumstances preclude the human need for affection, love, relationship, and physical intimacy of varying kinds.[4]

Weddings involving such couples take place in nursing institutions of all sorts as well as churches. Because of the physical circumstances that surround these weddings, topics for the preacher suggest themselves in several ways. The proclaimer may speak of the tensions between health and illness, the strong spirit of love, which "overcomes all," the issue of God's support and faithfulness to a marriage relationship that may only see worsening days, the presence of God in weakness, and the meaning of hope.

Care should be taken, whatever the topic(s), to neither hide nor gloss over obvious issues on the one hand, nor romanticize what is happening on the other. Again, the couple's thinking on these matters must be included for their own perceptions of what has brought them to the point of marrying in a possibly problematic context.

---

[4]James Nelson quotes a director of gerontological nursing, "Have you ever seen a double bed in an institution [of nursing care]?" in "The Sexually Disenfranchised," in James B. Nelson, *Embodiment: An Approach to Sexuality and Christian Theology* (Minneapolis: Augsburg, 1978), 211–35.

Conclusion

A theology of marriage, as reflected in a wedding sermon, depends on the pastor for its effectiveness and accuracy. Of particular importance in creating a theology of marriage, in both individual sermons and in all the pastor's wedding sermons, is the personal pastoral relationship established with each engaged couple. Honesty and the willingness to probe a variety of matters must typify this relationship from the pastoral point of view.

Out of such conversations, the essential components of a good wedding sermon contain a mix of scriptural text, appropriate topics, a keen awareness of concerns provided by the couple, and the ways these are formed into an appropriate theology of marriage within a given faith perspective. The key that will yield the decisive blending of these elements is a pastoral relationship with the marrying couple that finds expression in the wedding address.

Because marriage today happens with a diversity of lifestyles and situations, the preacher must successfully negotiate text choice, topics, and the peculiar instances of relationship presented by each couple. Denominational and personal theologies may be reconfigured, depending on what these circumstances are.

7

Wedding Sermon Structures
and Delivery

Wedding proclamation, both in structure and delivery, offers almost endless possibilities. This chapter will present some of the structural options and discuss these in relationship to delivery. One feature that is present in all the sermon outlines is termed "Introduction and Welcome." It is in this beginning portion of the sermon that the preacher must do all that is possible to involve, set at ease, and focus the community on what is unfolding. The pastor's sense of humor and occasion and graciousness are essential for any wedding sermon and service. This presence of the presider is more than a matter of ecclesial aesthetics; it befits the hospitality of Christ that is an implicit and explicit part of worship leadership.

The first priority in determining a sermon's structure is the preacher's decision about the approach of the sermon; in other words, what is the *intentionality* of the sermon? Is it encouragement? establishment of new directions? exhortation? thoughtful challenge? other? This selection of pastoral tone and approach will determine how the preacher balances and emphasizes different parts of the sermon.

The combination of topics, texts, and the possible social configurations of different marriages offers the preacher a variety of sermonic structural options. Given the multiplicity of elements in any wedding, these are listed in outline form only and without regard to priority. A scriptural textual basis may inform all of these approaches either implicitly or explicitly.

The following sermon outlines are arranged only as suggestions for the emphases in a sermon and not as strict outlines of the sermon, although they may be used in that fashion. The first outline reflects the explicit ancient historical thread of wedding sermon topics described in chapter 2.

> *Outline #1: Historical—Topical*
> I. Introduction and Welcome
>   II. Remembrances
>   III. Exhortations
>   IV. Blessings
>   V. Conclusion

This arrangement can use a given text, a topic from or related to the text, a textual metaphor, or a metaphor unique to the couple's lives and reflected through the text selection. A variant of this is specifically linked to a text(s).

> *Outline #2: Historical—Textual—Topical*
> I. Introduction and Welcome
>   II. (a) Text—Remembrances
>   III. (b) Text—Exhortations
>   IV. (c) Text—Blessings
>   V. Conclusion

There is a scripturally implicit approach for the strictly topical wedding sermon.

> *Outline #3: Topical*
> I. Introduction and Welcome
>   II. Couple
>   III. Topic
>   IV. Theologizing on Couple/
>   Topic
>   V. Conclusion

Another possible ordering of the sermon is strictly text-derived.

> *Outline #4: Scriptural Text/"Text" of the Couple*
>   I. Introduction and Welcome
>   II. Biblical Text
>   III. Couple in View of the Text
>   IV. God's Text/Our Text
>   V. Conclusion

The range of types of biblical texts, their lengths, and their connection with the marriage can assist the preacher in deciding whether to set the text side-by-side with the couple's own life text or whether to weave elements of each together throughout. This structure lends itself well to narrative portions of scripture and may combine several elements or topics.

A variant of this that works with the overtly theological elements of scripture, such as epistle selections, can follow this structure.

> *Outline #5: Weaving the Text and the Couple's Lives*
>   I. Introduction and Welcome
>   II. Text and Couple
>   III. Conclusion

Perhaps one of the most common approaches to the wedding homily is the topic derived from a text. Again, there are several possibilities.

> *Outline #6: Textual—Topical*
>   I. Introduction and Welcome
>   II. Text and Topic Named: Why These?
>   III. Text, Topic, and Couple
>   IV. Conclusion

Many wedding sermons are characterized by a collection of texts related to one or more topics.

> *Outline #7: Topical—Multiple Texts*
>   I. Introduction and Welcome
>   II. Text References—Topic

III. Summary of Topic—Couple—
Text(s)

A related approach is the identification of a governing or root metaphor. This can be worked in two ways, with the first using a specific text.

Outline #8: Metaphor a
I. Introduction and Welcome
II. A Textual Metaphor
III. Couple and Textual Metaphor
IV. Conclusion

This form may use a text only implicitly, or it may use a cluster of different texts containing the same metaphor.

Outline #9: Metaphor b
I. Introduction and Welcome
II. Couple and Metaphor
III. Theological Reflections on the
Metaphor
IV. Conclusion

Other possibilities include the use and division of a liturgical text. For example, in a wedding sermon that focuses on the topic of God's agape toward and with humanity, the minister can use three parts of the Apostles' Creed in the following manner:

Outline #10: Liturgical / Topical
I. Introduction and Welcome
II. God the Creator and Couple
III. God the Redeemer and Couple
IV. God the Comforter and Couple
V. Conclusion

Another liturgical possibility for the sermon is the use of the structure of a well-known hymn. The hymn should be used as part of the worship service, preferably close to the preaching. The preacher can even direct the congregation to sing the verse(s) prior to preaching about it. It is important not to omit verses in choosing a hymn, since many hymns tell a complete story through all the verses.

> *Outline #11: Hymnody—Topical*
> I. Introduction and Welcome
> II. Couple and Hymn:Verse(s) #_____
>   III. Couple and Hymn:Verse(s) #_____
>   IV. Couple and Hymn:Verse(s) #_____
>   V. Conclusion

Another general category of wedding sermon, with or without a textual basis and with or without a topical basis, is the use of a particular genre whose own structure provides the structure of the sermon. This includes such things as a poem, a story, a recipe, the description of a game, or a road map. It is important to be aware of the types of theology one provides in using other-than-scriptural or scripturally related genre and approaches.

The Threshold of Proclamation: Perspectives and Possibilities

Today's wedding sermons are available from several denominational sources and in a multiplicity of published forms, through homily and sermon subscription services and clergy who publish their own creative approaches to preaching. The following samples highlight a variety of desired emphases in wedding proclamation in different denominations. Homiletical directives, beyond the terms used to describe the preaching, are sometimes available. These descriptions are useful to the proclaimer for suggesting new possibilities in sermon structure as well as giving direction to those participating in ecumenical wedding ceremonies. For Lutherans, the *Manual on the Liturgy* says:

> An address may follow, commenting on the readings and giving a contemporary witness to the biblical understanding of marriage, stressing the foundation of the dependable love of God, the complete sharing that

is the essence of marriage, marriage as a sign of the kingdom.[1]

Roman Catholic sources give ample directions for preaching and specify the expectations in this way: After the gospel, the priest gives a homily drawn from the sacred text. He speaks about the

> mystery of Christian marriage, the dignity of wedded love, the grace of the sacrament, and the responsibilities of married people, keeping in mind the circumstances of this particular marriage.[2]

Methodists offer a description of the wedding sermon that greatly expands traditional definitions of the sermon.

> The purpose of a wedding sermon is to proclaim to the couple and to the congregation the Christian message of God's fidelity and what it means for the wedding and the beginning of a new life together. The sermon can proclaim the promise God gives to the union and God's act in making our union possible. Such a sermon is most effective if it is brief and to the point.
>
> The witness to Christian marriage at this point in the service may take many forms other than a sermon. One or more friends or family members may speak. The two charges at the beginning of the traditional service, or some other appropriate classical or contemporary reading, may be read as a homily. The proclamation may be choral or visual. It could be liturgical dance during readings or acts of praise.[3]

---

[1]Philip H. Pfaateicher and Carlos R. Messerli, *Manual on the Liturgy: Lutheran Book of Worship* (Minneapolis: Augsburg, 1979), 349.

[2]*Rites of Marriage* (New York: Catholic Book Publishing, 1970), 725.

[3]*The United Methodist Book of Worship* (Nashville: United Methodist Publishing, 1992).

These descriptions of the sermon or homily are important because they establish a certain range of topical priorities: They clearly identify theological topics, the role of scripture, and the context of the marriage for a given faith outlook. As such, they are factors that give significant shape to the structure of the wedding homily.

Public Proclamation

The threshold of the completed wedding sermon is at hand. How does the minister creatively blend pastoral knowledge of the couple, their context with appropriate topics, and texts for a finished sermon that is resonant with a given denominational theology of marriage?

First, the proclamatory genre of the wedding sermon is inevitably tied to other public components of the wedding. As noted earlier, the terminology of the genre includes "address," "homily," "message," or "sermon." For the sake of the worshiping public, a denominationally accurate word should be used in the bulletin describing the wedding proclamation.

A wedding sermon occurs only if the couple agrees to one and/or the preacher thinks it is a priority. Compared with other forms of proclamation, it tends to be brief. Many pastors say they preach no more than five or six minutes as a comfortable time frame. Others may claim as much as ten to thirteen minutes.

For those who wish to preach longer, there is a logistical reality involved. It is difficult for couples to stand for a long sermon. Participants may or may not wish to sit down, depending on what type of wedding garb they are wearing. If the pastor does intend to preach for a long period, arrangements should be made to seat the couple in the chancel, either together, side by side, or facing each other. It is unfair to the wedding party not to let them know what the sermon length may be. This may be very important for those who are physically challenged in any way or elderly.

Another way that pastors might officiate and proclaim is by facing the couple, standing on a lower level than they are;

again, this takes some creative seating arrangements so that none of the participants are totally blocked from congregational view.

Records of a wedding homily can be a pastoral gift to the couple. These days services are usually taped. The pastor may wish to give the couple a paper copy of the sermon as a gift.[4]

Another delivery matter has to do with whom the preacher is addressing. Wedding sermon audiences can be as multitiered as a wedding cake! The most obvious primary focus is the couple. Beyond that is the family and then the congregation as a whole. Phrasing, emphasis, and eye contact all come into play. Many pastors use the tactic of preaching to the couple combined with the sense of a larger group that "overhears" what is being said.

If there are any interpersonal issues readily apparent in the group (e.g., issues related to divorce, blended families, resistance to the event itself, etc.), it is essential that the pastor express sensitivity to this through appropriate language and other nonverbal elements of delivery.

It is particularly important that the proclaimer speak clearly and loudly enough for the entire congregation to hear. Frequently, it is easy to speak "sotto voce" so that only the couple hears most of the sermon. If the pastor is aware of the possible range of meanings wedding proclamations can have for the entire assembly, this should be kept in mind.

The manuscript of the wedding homily varies. Sometimes it may be read from a denominationally prescribed book. More often, the preacher will use a set of cards or notes. Since wedding sermons are often given outside the pulpit or lectern, it is important that such notes do not distract. The minister may want to keep them between the covers of the worship book or in a hardback folder; even a choir music folder will be adequate. The use of other books, such as an occasional service book, the bulletin, the handling of rings, and the laying on of

---

[4]I am indebted to Pastor Timothy Staveteig for this suggestion.

hands all make it crucial that the pastor create no problems with any paperwork associated with the homily.

While it is a small detail, this next item is perhaps the most important point of etiquette in the sermon. If a pastor preaches frequently at weddings to people with whom there is little acquaintance or familiarity, it is an excellent safeguard to type or write clearly in the sermon text the names of the couple marrying. Do not leave this to chance or memory!

Conclusion

Proclamatory presence must be established at the beginning of every wedding sermon through the preacher's efforts to graciously involve the congregation in its participation in the marriage service. The homiletical sense of hospitality created as a preface to all preaching enables the congregation to better listen to the sermon.

Because of the ever-changing nature of the audience/ listeners to a wedding sermon, the structures of the sermon can reflect numerous configurations reflective of materials that are biblical, liturgical, theological, topical, literary, and personal. Additionally, denominational wedding directives are a starting point for developing the wedding homily. They name the vocabulary used to describe the preaching and sometimes provide other foci that the minister should consider, such as intentionality, scriptural sources, topics, metaphors, extrabiblical materials, particular theology of marriage, and contextualized meaning of the sermon.

Delivery of the wedding sermon depends on the length of the sermon, the wishes of the officiating clergy, and the layout of the church itself. It is essential that the minister decide to which audience(s) the sermon will be aimed: the couple, the congregation present at the service, or the greater community extending beyond the parish.

8

"With Love": Sample Wedding Sermons

Several contemporary wedding sermons comprise this chapter, and they illustrate combinations of scripture, topics, and context well. All of these preachers vary in training, years in the ministry, venues of ministry, and faith perspectives. I am indebted to them for providing a written record from the personal heart of their ministry and faithful proclamation.

The first sermon is by Pastor Sheri Delvin, an Evangelical Lutheran Church in America pastor in Chicago. It is preached in a parish setting. She combines the 1 Corinthians 13 text with material from the Song of Songs. She shares her personal experience of marriage through the two interrelated topics of kindness and community. This sermon reflects the pastoral relationship with the couple in several loving ways.

The second sermon is from Fr. Walter J. Burghardt, S. J. Out of the pluralistic ministry setting of Georgetown University, Washington, D.C., he preaches to a couple who experience the joy and tension of an interfaith marriage. In this sermon Father Burghardt seeks, as a committed Christian, a common ground for such a marriage. He, too, includes the 1 Corinthians 12—13 text in connection with other texts on love.

The third sermon is an example of the contemporary pastoral crossroads at which so many preachers find themselves: How does one preach to those one cares deeply about but who represent a worldview radically different from that of the preacher? Is this sermon "Christian"? The reader must judge for her- or himself.

Certainly, the proclamation asserts a pastoral care perspective that reflects the preacher's faith and care for the couple and their families. For both the sake of the preacher and the marrying couple, this sermon is anonymous in terms of its personal details of authorship and wedding couple. The sermon is preached without a specific biblical text, although a particular theological approach is embedded within it.

Sermon four is a wedding homily preached by the Reverend Dr. Lucy Lind Hogan. It uses one biblical text and amplifies its meaning with a second one. This sermon reflects a bride, divorced and remarrying, and a groom who lost his wife to cancer. The former is Methodist, the latter Roman Catholic. Dr. Hogan is an ordained Episcopal priest and professor of preaching and worship at Wesley Theological Seminary in Washington, D.C.

Sermon five is by Dr. W. Sibley Towner of Union Theological Seminary, Richmond, Virginia. His sermon is based on the Song of Songs, a biblical book that offers rich yet little-used material for a wedding sermon. The sermon represents the best of what it means to preach incarnationally.

Depending on the pastoral decisions about privacy, details regarding the wedding service participants may be explicit, absent, or changed in the following sermons.

A Wedding Sermon
Pastor Sheri Delvin
1 Corinthians 13

It is the day! Two days ago as Dave and I spoke on the phone about the printing of the bulletins, he gave me the final changes and I said "It's a wrap—you can't change your mind now." Of course, meaning he couldn't change his mind about the service. But there was a considerable pause, and then he replied, "I wondered when that moment would be—when I would know there was no turning back." Well, Dave, it is now. And see what a beautiful day it is.

I know that everyone here knows how hard you two have worked to come to this day. Sometimes we wished that you would not have worked quite so hard and long. But it is to your credit that your love and this marriage is based on integrity. Integrity in marriage is the same as integrity in steel; if you don't have it, it doesn't matter what you do have.

You know that commitment is not simple, that love is not easy. You know that honoring each other means sometimes asking hard questions and giving hard answers. And you know that sometimes, maybe even most of the time, love, commitment, and honor mean that you will trust to live the questions because there are no answers.

You have chosen each other as traveling companions. You don't know the road, but you have chosen the way you will travel—with each other. And you can trust that the journey will be better, richer, and deeper because of that choice.

On this day you will make promises to each other, but there are no promises about how your life together will unfold—only that you will be with each other as it unfolds. That is the ancient promise made by our Creator to the beloved creatures and the promise of Jesus to his beloved friends: There is no promise of what life will be; but a promise that it will not be lived alone.

So dear ones, when the road seems long, when you feel lost, frightened, discouraged, confused, remember those who gather around you this day, for they have been sent by God so that you can turn to them and they can remind you of the promises of this day. And don't forget to share your joys. Because joy shared is always joy multiplied.

We are eager to share your joy now as you take your marriage vows.

There are two things I want to say to you that I have learned from being a Christian—a Christian who has been married for twenty-five years:

Love is more about kindness than we can imagine.

In the story about the rich young man, Jesus asks a young man a few religious questions. The young man gets the answers right. Then Jesus asks him a practical religious question that the young man cannot answer. He gets the answers right, but fails the test. But the story says, "Jesus looked on him with love." Each of you will have times when you will get the answers right and fail the test—many times you will miss the questions and not even know you are being tested!

Karen, if you can look on David with love at those times, you will know what love really is. David, if you can look on Karen with love at those times, you will know what love really is. When you can see each other at your most vulnerable and remember to love as if you were always at your most true and best self, you have learned how to love with kindness. It is not easy to do. You will constantly take turns loving each other into your truest and best selves. Sometimes you will even need to be reminded to be kind to each other, because kindness will be the last thing in your heart. Which brings me to the second thing I want to tell you.

Love at its deepest and truest happens in and through community.

You will need to be reminded to be kind to one another because the world so often isn't a place where kindness is valued. We talked a lot about the community of friends you have gathered around you today. How they have been so important to your growth, health, relationships. And it is true, we are not solitary creatures, and your marriage is not a solitary union. By gathering these friends around you, you are asking them to help you be accountable to your love for one another. Your love is not just your business—it is our business. I know that surprised you when we first talked about it. And I hope it is beginning to sound less strange, but not less serious.

Your ability to love each other with integrity is in large part due to the courage you have had to share your love with friends and family. They have encouraged you when you were despairing, been patient when you have misunderstood, and admonished you when you were less than your best selves. Those days are not over; they are beginning in earnest now. We are here because we love you and desire to be part of your life together. Honor us by continuing to include us in your married life; not just in the glorious times, but in the not so glorious ones too.

The text from Song of Songs [read earlier] is one lover's call to the other to be faithful. She claims that love is stronger than death, passion more powerful than the grave. Being faithful is more than sexual fidelity, although that is part of it. Faithfulness is remembering that you are marrying so that you can be partners in loving each other into your truest and best selves. Being faithful is remembering the intention of God that we live in community with one another so that we can know our truest and best selves. And finally, remember that God is ultimately faithful, so you can love each other freely and with faithfulness.

Amen.

Christ or Buddha?[1]
Father Walter J. Burghardt, S. J.
Genesis 1:26–28, 31; 1 Corinthians 12:31—13:8; John 15:9–12

Today we gather to celebrate. To celebrate love. The love of a man and a woman. There is always reason to celebrate such love. But today, I suggest, we have a special, singular reason

---

[1]Preached by Fr. Walter J. Burghardt, S.J., at the wedding of Cathy and Dien at Holy Trinity Church, Washington, D.C., on November 3, 1990. Reprinted by permission from "Christ and/or Buddha?" in *When Christ Meets Christ* (New York/Mahwah: Paulist Press, 1993), 98–102.

to rejoice, because today love unites a woman who is Roman Catholic and a man who is Buddhist. Cause for joy? I am acutely aware that to many of you this may sound strange; so let me expand on it in three stages. First, the differences that divide us. Second, the elements that unite us. Third, the role that Cathy and Dien will play in our lives. Let me speak very frankly to all of you here, because we are closer to one another than we think, but must come closer than we actually are.

I

First the differences that divide us. However much we try, a certain uneasiness hovers over a Catholic-Buddhist marriage. The backgrounds are so different. To begin with, Christ and Buddha seem so far apart: the eternal Son of God who was born of a virgin, lived a celibate existence, spent three years preaching repentance and rebirth and a kingdom not of this earth, and died in agony on a bloody cross; and the Buddha who married, renounced wife and child to seek deliverance from pain and rebirth, reached the stage of emptiness through asceticism, and attained "Enlightenment" by understanding suffering and the way to conquer it.

Again, the Catholic is brought up on a system of beliefs. Not that dogma alone can save; it cannot. But the system is terribly important for Catholics; untold thousands have died cruel deaths rather than forsake their faith. On the other hand, for all its reverence for sacred teachings, Buddhism is not a belief system in the Western sense. Buddhists "require of religion not that it be true rather than false, but that it be good rather than bad." Buddhism is doing—living this moment.

Again, as we move about the world, there is a recognizable sameness about Catholicism, despite the cultural clothes that, for example, distinguish an African Mass from an American one. But as we move from India to Sri Lanka, to Burma and Thailand, to Vietnam and Laos and Cambodia, to China and Tibet and Mongolia, to Korea and Japan, the variety of Buddhist beliefs and sects, monasteries and temples, traditions and worship, impressive though they are, understandably confuse us.

As we must confuse you with our insistence on a body of doctrine significant for salvation: one God in three persons, a dying/rising Son of God; a worship that centers on the body of Christ made present on our altars and in our bodies; a moral code that guides our living from bedroom to boardroom.

Our total cultures are so different. We look different, talk a different language, eat different foods, have different values. In consequence, we often feel uneasy in one another's presence; all too often we do not know what to say. We are such different people. Let's admit it, and start from there.

II

But, second, where do we go from there? We start with awareness: I mean, recognizing that we are closer than we think, have more in common than we realize. I, a Catholic, resonate to the Eightfold Path the Buddha formulated to overcome the desire that for him was the root of suffering in human existence. (1) You know the truth. (2) You intend to resist evil. (3) You say nothing to hurt others. (4) You respect life, morality, and property. (5) You hold a job that does not injure others. (6) You struggle to free your mind of evil and to embrace what is good. (7) You control your feelings and your thoughts. (8) You practice contemplation, concentration. In this way good men and women enjoy a remarkable freedom and endless bliss. Buddhists, for their part, can echo a strong amen to what Jesus called the two greatest commandments of the law: "You shall love the Lord your God with all your heart, and with all your soul, and with all your mind, and with all your strength... You shall love your neighbor as yourself" (Mark 12:30–31).

A Catholic, I can relate to the Buddhist stress on monastic life, with its insistence on poverty, meditation, and study. At the same time, I am drawn to the Buddhist ability to link contemplation with action, meditating and doing, eternal bliss and the supreme importance of the present moment.

On the other hand, I know that Buddhists can feel comfortable with much that triggers Catholic daily life. Our Ten

Commandments warn us against worshiping false gods, insist on reverence for parents, prohibit killing and stealing, adultery and false witness. We foster a profound respect for life, from the youngest fetus to the oldest of the aging. We are deeply concerned over issues of social justice: unethical business practices, the enslaving poverty that afflicts one of every five U.S. children, the rape of the earth, substance abuse, 35 million Americans without access to healthcare, minorities with second-class citizenship.

III

So then, we are closer than we think; still, we are not as close as we ought to be. This leads to my third and final point: the role of Cathy and Dien in our lives. Very simply, their love is the high point in our gathering, not only because these two individuals are joining hands and hearts, but because their love is a living symbol. Dien and Cathy symbolize the oneness that should exist between Buddhists and Catholics; they suggest without words the way we ought to see one another. Oh yes, they themselves do not see eye to eye on ever so many religious issues. But they are willing to join their individual lives, even their individual religions, in the conviction that their love will enable them to understand each other more intimately.

They are not mouthing the absurd aphorism "Love conquers all." No, love simply cannot overcome all problems raised by cultures and beliefs. But without love no serious effort can be made to decrease the distance that separates—separates nations and peoples, Catholic and Protestant, atheist and Jew, yes Christian and Buddhist. Without love we will not take the trouble to understand one another. And without understanding we live dreadfully isolated lives, live on the edge of tragedy, personal, national, universal. I recall vividly how a thoughtful journalist, Meg Greenfield, many years ago added a new dimension to explain America's tragic failure in Vietnam: We did not really know who the Vietnamese were. If love increases understanding, conversely understanding deepens love. It is a constant movement back and forth, like a pendulum that never stops.

That is why this religious ceremony, what Catholics call the eucharist, is so important, even if some of you do not relate to it. For the eucharist reenacts what Catholics see as the most remarkable love in human history, the love that brought God's Son down to earth to share our flesh, to walk our way, to experience our pain, to die our death. And he did all this for reasons the original Buddha, Siddhartha Gautama, would understand: to free us from enslavement to worldly desires, to bring an enlightenment that would pierce through the unhappiness of human existence, to deal a deathblow to death, to make possible perfect peace and happiness.

Knowing all this, we shall still be different; for we understand in different ways, we search for an ultimate truth, a final love, that is a mystery, that neither Buddhist nor Catholic can comprehend in our present stage of light-with-darkness. But we will be ever so much closer, because we shall be searching together, in sympathy with one another.

Cathy and Dien: Although I have not addressed you directly, I trust you have sensed that you are central to all I have said. For in a few moments your exchange of vows will not only bind you together for life in a unique personal relationship of love; it will lay on you a singular privilege, an uncommon burden. You see, the love and understanding you bring to each other must leap out to us, to Buddhists and Catholics—in fact, to all whose lives you will touch. The way the two of you look at each other in love, this should rub off on the rest of us.

It is not a mission impossible. The proof? This homily. You two have compelled me to look deeply inside myself, to regret my own neglect of Buddhism, to discover some of its religious riches. Strangely—or not so strangely—I am a better Catholic for the experience, much richer, if only because I have seen the hand of God outstretched over all the earth, have found the love of the Lord in ways of thinking foreign to mine.

Finally, I urge all of you to open your minds and hearts to the three texts just read to you from the Christian scriptures. Three memorable affirmations. (1) All of us have been shaped in God's image, are like God. Male and female, Christian and Buddhist, we are gifted with the power to know and to love; we share God's own understanding, God's own freedom. (2) All of us are challenged by Saint Paul's lyrical outbursts to the Christians of Corinth: "If I…understand all mysteries and all knowledge, and if I have all faith, so as to remove mountains, but do not have love, I am nothing. If I give away all my possessions, and if I hand over my body so that I may boast, but do not have love, I gain nothing" (1 Cor. 13:2–3). (3) All of us can resonate to the words of a man who died for every single one of us: "'This is my commandment, that you love one another as I have loved you'" (Jn. 15:12).

Wedding of Karina and Roger
an Anonymous Pastor

Karina and Roger, I hope you feel the joy that fills all our hearts today and our gratitude for providing the occasion that makes it possible for all of us to be here.

Last night Roger told us how, almost two years ago to the day, the two of you met in the low-ceiling kitchen of a run-down house in Cleveland. But even this graphic description of that encounter couldn't domesticate my sense of marvel at the force of fate that, like some powerful magnet, spanned a continent and drew together a Hispanic woman from Arizona and a French Canadian man from Montreal.

What is this mysterious power that unites two people who lived most of their lives without knowing the other even existed? Well, in the lines of the poem that she read a few minutes ago, Jan named it love: "It is love that fashions us…and ultimately shapes us." And this afternoon I want to make two simple statements about love that, on the surface, may seem contradictory: LOVE IS POWERFUL and LOVE IS VULNERABLE.

Love, of course, comes in many varieties. There's the love I may have for my present job or car; the love of parent for child and friend for friend; the love of a woman and a man for each other. And the Greeks had a word for every one of these forms of love, though we do not.

But there's another form of love that gathers up and then transcends all these other forms. The Greeks called it *agape*. It's the love that, without thought of cost or reward, offers itself totally for the good of others. It's a love all too rare in our world, and it's because of its rarity that we honor Jesus above Caesar, and Ghandi, and Martin Luther King, Jr., above all the power brokers of our century. There seemed to pour through these lives, and those of others we could name, a loving power and a powerful love that flows from the hidden Source of all life, the secret Ground of our being.

And, Karina and Robert, it's this self-giving, other-affirming love that we covet for you today and through all the years ahead. It will move you to consider the other ahead of yourself and will teach you to be more skilled at giving than receiving. Such love will be patient, kind, gentle, caring, and in the words of one who meditated deeply on the meaning of love, it will be "love that endures." That is, it will outlast the years and all the unknown chances and changes the years are sure to bring. It will be able to conquer even conflict and pain and forge them into bonds that hold you together more closely that before. So, LOVE IS POWERFUL…beyond all the other powers we esteem so highly today.

———————

But it must also be said that LOVE IS VULNERABLE. To say that love is at the same time enduring, fragile, powerful, and vulnerable isn't a contradiction but a paradox. In fact, love is powerful precisely because it is vulnerable. And if it were not vulnerable, it wouldn't be love.

Love is vulnerable because it lures us out of our hiding places and forces us into the open arena of life. It requires of us the risk of exposing ourselves, "warts and all," to the knowledge of another who might reject us because of our flaws and frailties.

At the same time, it leads us to invite into our lives another who also brings along flaws and frailties that plead for understanding and acceptance. This is why marriage, which is love's public commitment, is a venture for which no angels need apply, but only imperfect, incomplete human beings like ourselves.

This makes the joining of two loving and loved persons like yourselves a task as well as a gift. The beautiful but fragile flower of love requires careful and constant tending. It survives only in the deep soil of faithfulness and trust. It needs the daily nourishment of tolerance of differences, open communication, mutual encouragement, and the sharing of both joy and pain. Above all, it requires an unwillingness to ever turn your face away from the other and a readiness to take the first step toward the other when love has been wounded.

Those of us who have walked or are walking this road know that it's a journey not to be undertaken alone. But this gathering around you today of family and friends is a signal to you that you're surrounded and upheld by a network of love—persons who will be slow to intrude into your lives but quick to respond when needed and asked.

And there's something more; a power of Love, unseen but present in this vast and wonderful universe—the hidden Source of all our human loves, hovering around you and available to you.

So, though I don't think either of you has a drop of Irish blood running through your veins, I want to close with an ancient Celtic blessing:

May the sun of God's love ever shine over you;
May the road rise up straight before you; and
May the wind of the Spirit be always at your back.

The Call to Love One Another: The Wedding of Terry and Jennie Hogan; 21 August, 1994
the Reverend Dr. Lucy Lind Hogan
John 15:9–12

It is such an honor for me to be asked to officiate at the marriage of Jennie and Terry. I did have one major concern when Terry and Jennie invited me to celebrate. I always cry at the weddings of people I love, so I was concerned that I would not be able to get through the wedding. (So far so good, but it is not over yet!)

In the portion of John's gospel that was just read, Jesus invites us to "abide in [his] love" (Jn. 15:9b). Abide in love. What does that mean? How can we abide in God's love? We abide in love when we know that we have been created by a God who loves us. We are able to abide in God's love when we remember and know, deep in our hearts, that we have been brought out of sin and death by a God who loves us. We abide in love when we know that we are sustained, strengthened, and nourished daily by the spirit of a loving God. Love is a giving of one to the other, grounded in mutual respect, concern, and affection.

Jesus offers us the invitation to "abide in his love." But he also issues us a command. We, who are God's creatures, are called to love one another with a love that approximates God's love for us. That would seem to be the easiest commandment to follow—to love one another. After all, have we not been created in the image of a loving God? Should we not be able to love one another? Yet this is perhaps the most difficult command we have been given.

Unfortunately, we need only to look at the world around us to discover that we have a long way to go before fulfilling that commandment. But, thanks be to God, we are given glimpses of what is possible when we abide in God's love, glimmers of grace that give us hope. Into our lives come moments when God's love shines through the darkness, and we are all transformed. Terry and Jennie's wedding is one of these moments.

We have come together in this place to share in their joy and celebration and to remind them that we will support them as they begin a new life together. In the Anglican church we consider marriage to be a sacramental rite. That means that we understand that the vows of love and the pledge of commitment and trust that Terry and Jennie make to one another are outward and visible signs of the inward, unseen, but still very real, spiritual grace of God's love for them and for all of us. Marriage is important, not just for the people who are married, not just for Jennie and Terry, but for all people. Marriage both reminds us of God's call to love one another and gives us an example of that love in the flesh.

In his letter to the Christian community in Corinth the apostle Paul paints a portrait of Godly love. Paul tells us that love is not a state of being. Love is not a passive verb. No, love is an active verb. Love is reaching out to one another with care and compassion, with a love that is both patient and kind. When we love someone with Godlike love, he writes, we are not arrogant or rude, we are not self-centered, but we place the other at the very center of our complete attention. We celebrate when they succeed, and we commiserate when they fail. We are there in times of both sickness and health.

We who are gathered here today have gone through many things together. We have laughed in times of joy and success. We have shed many tears together during long and painful moments. And we know that it was both God's love and the love and support of one another that helped us through those difficult times.

When we live in God's love and love others with that same love, together we are able to bear all that life will give us. Then we are able to believe that all things are possible and have hope for the future.

Love puts our lives in perspective. Paul reminded the church at Corinth that, even if you can prophesy and have faith strong enough to move mountains, but have no love—then you are nothing. We might have status and fame, power, money, intelligence, but if we do not acknowledge the love that God has offered us, or open ourselves to the love of others, then we are nothing.

Today we witness to God's healing love, God's strengthening love, God's call for life to go on. We are saying yes to life. Terry and Jennie, your marriage is a sign of God's love for us. I pray that we may let this important moment in the lives of Terry and Jennie serve as a reminder to all of us of God's love and God's call to love others. For remember, Paul tells us, when the power and riches of this world are gone, when buildings fall and mountains crumble, only faith, hope, and love will abide, and the greatest of these is love.

Love
the Reverend Dr. W. Sibley Towner
Song of Songs 7:10–13; 1:14; 8:6–7 (author's paraphrase)

Dear friends, there is a passage of scripture which I would like to read out over your wedding. Listen:

I am my beloved's,
And his desire is for me.
Come, my beloved,
Let us go forth into the fields,
And lodge in the villages;
Let us go out early to the vineyards,
And see whether the vines have budded,
Whether the grape blossoms have opened
And the pomegranates are in bloom.
There I will give you my love.

The mandrakes give forth fragrance,
And over our doors are all choice fruits,
New as well as old,
Which I have laid up for you, O my beloved…
Make haste, my beloved,
And be like a gazelle
Or a young stag
Upon the mountains of spices…
Set me as a seal upon your heart,
As a seal upon your arm;…
Many waters cannot quench love,
Neither can floods drown it.
If a man offered for love
All the wealth of his house,
It would be utterly scorned.
(Song 7:10–13; 1:14, 8:6–7)

The "Trivial Pursuit" buffs here will recognize this scripture as a passage from the Song of Solomon, or Canticles. You may also recognize that Jews and Christians have hardly ever known what to do with this strange Old Testament book. Well, here is what we should do with it. We should read it at weddings! That is its original life-setting; it is a nuptial poem, intended to be recited at ancient oriental ceremonies, which took a lot longer than ours do, and give the troubadours and harp players plenty of time to linger over its more luscious phrases. It is a poem celebrating erotic love—and there's a theme that is appropriate for such occasions as this, not only for the bride and groom, but for the entire community here assembled.

Of course, the church always nervously tried to convert the plain meaning of the song through the device of allegory into a love song of Christ and the church. For example, in commenting on the verse

Your navel is a rounded bowl
That never lacks mixed wine.
Your belly is a sheaf of wheat,
Encircled with lilies. (Song 7:2)

the Westminster Assembly taught that this was reference to the two sacraments, the navel being the baptismal font, and the belly the Lord's supper.

We've got the Song of Solomon safely back from such distant places, and now we can make it a part of your wedding. Be human, give your relationship all you've got. Be unabashedly enthusiastic about each other; enjoy the garden where the lilies grow; enjoy your physical relationship for as long as you can, which is, believe it or not, until death parts you!

But there is more. Listen once again to the last verse:

Many waters cannot quench love,
Neither can floods drown it.
If a man [and let me add, or a woman]
Offered for love
All the wealth of his [or her] house,
It would be utterly scorned. (8:7)

This most profound verse of the entire Song of Solomon sets an out-of-sight price tag upon love. Compared to true love, an offer of an entire estate of wealth is just laughable nonsense, rightly to be scorned. "Love is strong as death," says another verse (v. 6), "many waters cannot quench [it]."

No doubt you agree. Any kind of love—erotic love, brotherly and sisterly love, self-giving love—is of inestimable worth. Yet all around us we see love fading away; we see it being quenched not by floods but by mere drops of discontent, or by little bitty buckets of boredom. We see people trading their love for far less than the wealth of their whole house, but for a mess of pottage. Why? I don't know. I don't pretend to see clearly the great sweep of cultural change in which we are all caught up. But this much I do know and I leave with you on your wedding day. The love that endures and that can be fully realized is in sickness and in health, in poverty and in riches, in sexual relations and in intellectual relations, in childbearing and in retirement, in that love that demands nothing in return. It hopes, of course, but does not demand. It is that love that does not ask "How am I doing?" but simply does. It is that love that wastes no time looking in the mirror, but gazes into the eyes of the other. Saints and psychiatrists alike (and even those who are both) confirm this—it's not what you get, but what you give that makes you a real and enduring lover. Such love "bears all things, believes all things, hopes all things, endures all things" (1 Cor. 13:7), though not in some sheep-like way, not without honest differences, not without open confrontations and even rip-snorting fights.

Such love comes clean to itself about everything that gets in the way of giving. Such love doesn't even expect too much of itself; no superhuman heroism, just steady reaching out.

Once I asked my mother-in-law how many sermons she had heard preached at weddings over her ninety-six years, and she said, "Maybe two or three." But she added, "One of them was at my own." Then she quoted a line from it. The preacher said, "Fred, if you ever get furious with Josephine, go out and split some wood for the stove. Josephine, if you ever get furious with Fred, go bake him an apple pie on that stove."

That is good love. It is the love that can be human, that can get hungry, that can get angry, but that can finally also put the responsibility for being a good lover exactly where it belongs—right here, on oneself. And believe me:

> If a man [or a woman] offered for [this kind of] love
> All the wealth of his [or her] house,
> It would be utterly scorned. (Song 8:7)

Amen.

Appendix A
Texts for Weddings

There are numerous types of poetry and prose suitable for wedding sermon use. Preachers can access these sources on the Internet, at local libraries and using interlibrary loan, or through the wealth of their own bookshelves. Marrying couples may also contribute extrabiblical texts for pastoral consideration.

Poetry

W. H. Auden
e. e. cummings
James Dickey
Emily Dickinson
T. S. Eliot
Lawrence Ferlinghetti
Robert Frost
Langston Hughes
Galway Kinnell
Stanley Kunitz
Denise Levertov
Audre Lorde
Marge Piercy
Adrienne Rich
Theodore Roethke
William Shakespeare (sonnets and play excerpts)
Dylan Thomas
Walt Whitman

Prose

Annie Dillard
Antoine de Saint-Exupéry, *The Little Prince*
Robert Fulghum
Dag Hammarskjöld, *Markings*
Omar Khayyám, *The Rubáiyát*

D. H. Lawrence
Madeline L'Engle
C. S. Lewis
Thomas Moore
Flannery O'Connor
M. Scott Peck
The classics of Western spirituality
Various ethnic collections of literature, including
    folktales and creation stories
Sermons from various collections

Miscellaneous

Excerpts from the following materials can be incorporated into wedding sermons: plays, children's books, recipes, riddles, proverbs, liturgical dance, and music of different types. Audiovisual materials may be used, such as slides, movies, or tapes. Objects related to the visual arts—sculpture, paintings, banners, pottery, tapestry, personal creations—are useful if pertinent. They can either be incorporated into the sermon in some fashion or used as nonverbal, visual backdrops. Care should be taken that any such items are clearly visible to the entire congregation.

One series that is very helpful is Bill Moyers' *Language of Life*. This is in hardcover or on eight videocassettes (New York: Bantam Dell, 1995). An example of one quote from this collection is from Jelaluddin Rumi, thirteenth-century Islamic mystic:

I am so small.
How can this great love
Be inside me?

Look at your eyes.
They're small.
Yet, they see
Enormous things.

Appendix B
Themes in Marriage

The following information was developed out of the joint counseling practice of Dr. Norma Schweitzer Wood and Dr. Herbert W. Stroup, Jr., Marriage and Family Counseling Associates in York, Pennsylvania. The former is currently an instructor in counseling at Lutheran Theological Seminary at Gettysburg and dean of the Seminary. The latter is retired professor emeritus from the same seminary.

The themes detailed below by Wood and Stroup are useful for discussion in marital counseling, and the minister may also find ample material therein for premarital counseling as well as possible suggestions for wedding sermon materials.

Four Themes in Marriage

Every marriage is, in some sense, unique, a complexity of its partners' beliefs, needs, and values. The overall goal for the couple and their pastor is to ferret through the maze of hopes and disappointments, to hear the basic, or core, issues in each person's story. For out of all that is spoken, the essential must be sifted from the incidental: Future hopes must be teased out from past hurts; what is real must be distinguished from what is only imagined.

To guide the couple in this refining process, the pastor looks for patterns within his or her situation to aid in understanding possibilities for change. An initial task in pastoral marriage counseling is to achieve a focus on the basic or core problems. Asking the couple is a direct way of getting to the task, but what comes out, usually, is a conglomeration of feelings, memories, situations, and frustrations, all tumbling on each other. Out of this heap, clarity and order had best emerge: The underlying problems need to be identified and addressed.

But how?

Embedded in couples' stories can be discerned the dramatic variants on four basic themes: security, intimacy, power, and freedom. These run like subplots through the relationship story, giving certain twists, turns, and foreshadows of denouement. These four existential themes may be expressed clearly and directly. "Since the beginning of our marriage, I've wanted to be closer to her but have always felt her putting up a guard," states one husband about his longing for marital intimacy. Or the themes may be present covertly, in veiled and coded ways, with partners acting out personal scripts in marital drama. Nonetheless, whatever occurs within marriage may find its expression under one or more of these themes.

Security, Intimacy, Power, and Freedom: At Work in Marriage

How, then, do these themes function in marriage?

First, as expressions of "perceived" or "felt" needs, they motivate attitudes and patterns of marital behavior as each partner tries to shape the marital world in an order that matches personal standards of normality, worth, and sense of fit. While a couple's debate might appear to be strictly about how money should be spent or how a child should be treated, these debates are fueled, less overtly, at a motivational level. A wife's need for security, for example, may come out in viewpoints toward the family budget, just as strongly as does her husband's need for freedom. Her experience of near-poverty in her family of origin may contribute to her need for financial security, while his relationship with strict parents drives him away from budget limitations and toward free spending. Their money conflict can be more productively addressed as they are helped to examine their behavior as expressions of these felt needs.

Second, the themes serve as values as well as felt needs. Sometimes the two are conflated or confused, so that a partner may say "I need you to do this with me," and actually mean "I would like you to because such and such is important to me." Out of the family culture and each person's other life-learnings develop values given to each theme. A partner may give more weight to intimacy than to freedom, or value security more than freedom, power more than security, and so on. A couple may deliberately give up certain securities in the service of certain altruistic values they hold. Values, then, have the potential to shape and transform psychological "needs."

Third, the themes have valence, that is, degrees of intensity. Both partners may give intimacy priority as a relationship theme, but one of them does so more intensely than the other. He or she puts forth great effort to achieve or protect that which has the higher valence. Moreover, a theme valence is subject to change as the couple copes with life events. For example, security needs usually intensify in times of crisis, as partners struggle with experiences of loss and hardship.

Fourth, the themes may operate in a marriage either fluidly or statically. In some relationships a spouse expresses them in a fixed, rigid manner. "This is the way I am. You knew this about me when you married me." In such marriages, the partner may conform to these needs and values, and after fifteen or more years the established marital pattern has undergone no significant change. In most instances, however, the themes are clearly influenced by the partner and by life events. The couple may experience positive change and growth with one another, or, conversely, they may move apart and polarize within the relationship.

Finally, as blends of felt need and value, the themes in relationship are always subjectively defined. As such, they may operate in what would be considered normal desires and hopes, or they may actually serve the relationship pathologically: Intimacy can be subverted into smothering, or power into sadistic domination, or freedom into sociopathy, and so on.

The Themes at Work in the Marital Counseling Process

If what people seek in marriage are variants of these four themes—security, intimacy, power, and freedom—the starting task in pastoral marriage counseling is to discern their patterned operations in the couple's relationship. To this end the themes are used diagnostically, so to speak, to make sense of marital history and the couple's present distress, to guide the process of exploration, and to discover directions for change.

Since pastoral marriage counseling is interested in faith perspectives as well as psychological ones, the diagnostic themes serve as a conceptual bridge between these two worlds.

For diagnostic purposes, then, each of the four themes is constructed as a continuum of definition and practice. Not unlike the readings on a thermometer, which place hot at one end of the scale and cold at the other, the theme continua, too, stretch from one relationship extreme to another. On the cool end are definitions of the theme in which a spouse is too autonomous in the relationship; on the hot end are definitions in which the partner is overinvolved. At the overinvolved end of the intimacy continuum, for example, might be the spouse who conceives of intimacy as uncensored openness and total sharing of thoughts and feelings. At the overautonomous end might be the spouse who thinks of intimacy in terms of very limited marital involvement, expecting no more than the evening meal together. In between these two conceptions lies a spectrum of personal definitions and leanings. Just so, with the other continua extremes, a person's drive for security, power, or freedom moves toward overautonomy at one end or overinvolvement at the other end.

From a psychological perspective, however, not all personal definitions are appropriate to a particular marital context. If, for example, a definition of intimacy fails to recognize the partner as a separate person, the relationship can be described as dysfunctional. Or if a definition fails to include a goal of mutual engagement, again, the relationship is not functional. These endpoints on each of the four continua, then, mark where a definition moves into dysfunction.

From a theological perspective, not all subjective definitions can be viewed as "faithful." Partners may view marriage entirely as a legal or social contract, or they may view marriage as a covenant of faith. Caught in values of self-interest, they may overlook or disregard what the Christian faith communicates about values related to power, freedom, intimacy, and security. The four themes, as described in models of continua, allow for and even promote movement in the counseling process from exploration to examination of a faith perspective on their lives and relationship. Each model reflects a spectrum, left to right from overautonomy to overinvolvement.

Security

Security as a motivational theme in marriage is derived from the desire for and the need to be safe, that is, to be relatively free from threat.

SECURITY

Fight Chaos with Good Order				Flight into Dependence on Partner
		Relative Absence of Threat		
Anxiety	Fear of Chaos		Fear of Abandonment	Anxiety

On the left, one seeks personal and interpersonal safety by the establishment of good order in his or her world. The ordering is carried out apart from its impact on the partner or on the relationship. At the right pole, one tries to find safety and relief from threat by entrusting the tasks of self-care and comfort to the partner. In the functional center, partners are able to manage anxiety through an appropriate mix of tolerance, self-reliance, and realistic trust in the partner's commitment to the relationship's life.

Intimacy

Intimacy as a motivational theme in marriage is derived from the desire for communion with a chosen partner. It seeks confirmation of the "I's" lovability and a transcending experience of "We."

Intimacy

Isolation	Individuality	Togetherness Ego Fusion
Disengagement	Engagement	Enmeshment

At the left pole, ego boundaries are rigid and impermeable, resulting in emotional isolation from the partner. At the right, ego boundaries are lost: Individual thoughts, feelings, and experiences between the two partners are undifferentiated and confused. In the functional center is a balance of individuality and togetherness. The "We" and the "I" are preserved with respect for partner differentness and by the partner's mutual desire for closeness in the relationship.

Power

Power as a motivational theme in marriage is derived from the desire to have effectiveness, to have a personal impact on the partner and on the relationship, and to have means to bring about chosen goals.

Power

	Competitive Manipulative		Nurturant Manipulative	
Power Over/ Exploitative	——————— (Aggressive)	Shared	——————— (Passive)	Powerless

At the left pole, dominance of the spouse by a partner is used to try to achieve personal goals. The concentration of power is self-serving. At the right, the spouse senses no power within the relationship. He or she experiences the self as acted upon, without means to move toward personal or relationship goals. In the functional center, partners view power synergistically, a sharing of means and resources.

Freedom

Freedom as a motivational theme in marriage joins choice with responsibility. It represents an interaction between desires for self-actualization and interpersonal responsibility.

FREEDOM

Choice: Responsibility

Choice (without responsibility)				Responsibility (without choice)
Narcissism	Child	Adult	Parent	Scrupulosity

At the left extreme, individual choice is practiced without a proportional sense of responsibility. At the right, a magnified perception of responsibility brings on an inordinate sense of responsibility. In the functional center, freedom and responsibility operate in tandem.

The Themes: Pastoral Perspective

The four diagnostic continua can be used to assist the pastor and couple in several important ways. First, they can be used by the pastor to bring out, as well as understand, in an ordered fashion, each partner's subjective experience within the marriage. Second, by presenting a continuum of definition, the constructs provide help for the couple to reflect on their marriage. They enable the couple's participation in assessing their own relationship's functional and dysfunctional aspects. Moreover, a continuum gives the couple a referential context not just to each other, but to a wider spectrum of human experience. Third, each of the constructs provides a bridge connecting the psychological and theological worlds, enabling the pastor and couple to move between faith's realities and psychological dynamics.

Appendix C
Denominational Lists of
Wedding Scriptures

The following lists are suggested texts for wedding ceremonies—possibly sermons—from the most recent Lutheran, Episcopal, Roman Catholic, Presbyterian, and Methodist sources. The texts are grouped, in each instance, from the oldest to the newest scripture readings. Scriptural sources are from many genres of biblical literature: mythic, wisdom, lyric, epistolary, gospel, and apocalyptic.

These lists are not only suggestive of the theological foci of marriage in each denomination, but can be useful to those who will preach at interdenominational wedding services.

Lutheran[1]
Psalms and Lessons

Psalm 33
Psalm 100
Psalm 117
Psalm 127
Psalm 128
Psalm 136
Psalm 150
The earth is full of the goodness of the Lord. (Ps. 33:5)
Happy are they who delight in the commandments of the
    Lord. (Ps. 112:1)
They are no longer two but one. (Mt. 19:6)
Genesis 1:26–31
Genesis 2:18–24
Song of Solomon 2:10–13
Song of Solomon 8:7

---

[1]"Notes on the Service," in *Occasional Services* (Minneapolis: Augsburg, and Philadelphia: Board of Publication, Lutheran Church in America, 1982), 31.

Isaiah 63:7–9
Matthew 19:4–6
John 2:1–10
John 15:9–12
Romans 12:1–2
1 Corinthians 12:31—13:13
Ephesians 5:21–33
Philippians 4:4–7
1 John 4:7–12

Episcopal[2]

Genesis 1:26–28
Genesis 2:4–9, 15–24
Song of Solomon 2:10–13; 8:6–7
Tobit 8:5b–8

1 Corinthians 13:1–13
Ephesians 3:14–19
Ephesians 5:1–2, 21–33
Colossians 3:12–17
1 John 4:7–16

Appropriate Psalms are 67, 127, and 128.

Matthew 5:1–10
Matthew 5:13–16
Matthew 7:21, 24–29
Mark 10:6–9 or 1–16
John 15:9–12

---

[2]"The Celebration and Blessing of a Marriage," in *The Book of Common Prayer* (New York: Church Hymnal Corporation and Seabury Press, 1979), 426.

Roman Catholic[3]

I. Old Testament

Genesis 1:26–28, 31a
Genesis 2:18–24
Genesis 24:48–51, 58–67
Tobit 7:9–10, 11–15
Tobit 8:5–10
Song of Songs 2:8–10, 14, 16a; 8:6–7a
Ecclesiasticus 26:1–4, 16–21 (Greek 1–4, 13–16)
Jeremiah 31:32a, 33–34a

II. New Testament Readings

Romans 8:31b–35, 37–39
Romans 12:1–2, 9–18 (longer) or Romans 12:1–2, 9–13
    (shorter)
1 Corinthians 6:13c–15a, 17–20
1 Corinthians 12:31—13:8a
Ephesians 5:2a, 21–33 (longer) or 2a, 25–32 (shorter)
Colossians 3:12–17
1 Peter 3:1–9
1 John 3:18–24
1 John 4:7–12
Revelation 19:1, 5–9a

III. Responsorial Psalms

Psalm 33:12 and 18, 20–21, 22
Psalm 34:2–3, 4–5, 6–7, 8–9
Psalm 103:1–2, 8 and 13, 17–18a
Psalm 112:1–2, 3–4, 5–7a, 7bc–8, 9
Psalm 128:1–2, 3, 4–5
Psalm 145:8–9, 10 and 15, 17–18
Psalm 148:1–2, 3–4, 9–10, 11–12ab, 12c–14a

---

[3]"Rite for Celebrating Marriage During Mass," in *The Rites of the Catholic Church*, vol. 1 (New York: Pueblo, 1990), 746–49.

IV. Alleluia Verse and Verse before the Gospel

1 John 4:8 and 11
1 John 4:12
1 John 4:16
1 John 4:7b

V. Gospels

Matthew 5:1–12
Matthew 5:13–16
Matthew 7:21, 24–29 (longer) or 21, 24–25 (shorter)
Matthew 19:3–6
Matthew 22:35–40
Mark 10:6–9
John 2:1–11
John 15:9–12
John 15:12–16
John 17:20–26 (longer) or 20–23 (shorter)

Presbyterian[4]

I. Old Testament

Genesis 1:26–31
Genesis 2:18–24
Song of Solomon 8:6–7
Proverbs 3:3–6
Isaiah 54:5–8
Jeremiah 31:31–34

II. Psalms

Psalm 8
Psalm 67, 95:1–7
Psalm 100
Psalm 103:1–5, 15–18
Psalm 117

---

[4]"Order for the Public Worship of God: The Marriage Service," in *Book of Common Worship* (Louisville: Westminster/John Knox Press, 1993), 893–94.

Psalm 121
Psalm 128
Psalm 136:1–9, 26
Psalm 145
Psalm 148
Psalm 150

III. Epistles

Romans 12:1–2, 9–18
1 Corinthians 13:1–13
Colossians 3:12–17
1 John 4:7–12
Revelation 19:1, 5–9

IV. Gospels

Matthew 5:1–10
Matthew 5:13–16
Matthew 19:3–6
Mark 10:6–9
John 2:1–11
John 15:1–17

Methodist[5]

I. Old Testament

Genesis 1:26–31
Song of Solomon 2:10–13, 8:6–7
Isaiah 43:1–7
Isaiah 55:10–13
Isaiah 61:10—62:3
Isaiah 63:7–9

---

[5]*Companion to the Book of Services: Introduction, Commentary, and Instructions for Using the New United Methodist Services,* Supplemental Worship Resource 17 (Nashville: Abingdon Press, 1988), 109–10.

II. Epistle

Romans 12:1, 2, and 9–18
1 Corinthians 12:31—13:8a
1 Corinthians 13
2 Corinthians 5:14–17
Ephesians 2:4–10
Ephesians 4:1–6
Ephesians 4:25—5:2
Philippians 2:1–12
Philippians 4:4–9
Colossians 3:12–17
1 John 3:18–24
1 John 4:7–16
Revelation 19:1, 5–9a

III. Gospel

Matthew 5:1–10
Matthew 7:21, 24–27
Matthew 22:35–40
Mark 2:18–22
Mark 10:42–45
John 2:1–11
John 15:9–17

Before or after readings, there may be appropriate hymns, psalms, canticles, anthems, or other music. Psalms 23, 33, 34, 37, 67, 103, 112, 145, or 150 (or hymns paraphrasing them) are suggested.

Bibliography

Books

Ayers, Tess, and Brown, Paul. *The Essential Guide to Lesbian and Gay Weddings*. San Francisco: Harper, 1993.

Barnard, Mary. *Sappho: A New Translation*. Berkeley: University of California Press, 1962.

Batey, Richard A. *New Testament Nuptial Imagery*. Leiden: E. J. Brill, 1971.

Biddle, Percy. *Abingdon Marriage Manual*. Rev. ed. Nashville: Abingdon Press, 1987.

Bonhoeffer, Dietrich. "A Wedding Sermon from a Prison Cell." In *Letters and Papers from Prison*. New York: Macmillan, 1953.

Book of Common Worship. Louisville: Westminster/John Knox Press, 1993.

Boswell, John. *Same Sex Unions in Premodern Europe*. New York: Villard Books/Random House, 1994.

Burghardt, Walter J., S.J. *Preaching: The Art and the Craft*. Mahwah, N.J.: Paulist Press, 1987.

Butler, Becky, ed. *Ceremonies of the Heart: Celebrating Lesbian Unions*. Seattle: Seal Press, 1990.

Calvin, John. "Form and Manner of Celebrating Marriage." In *Tracts and Treatises on the Doctrine and Worship of the Church*. Translated by Henry Beveridge, with historical notes by Thomas F. Torrance. Grand Rapids, Mich.: Eerdmans, 1958.

————. *Institutes of the Christian Religion*. The Library of Christian Classics. Vol. XXI (Books III.XX to IV. XX), section 34–37. Edited by John T. McNeill. Translated by Ford Lewis Battles. Philadelphia: Westminster Press, 1960.

Catullus, Gaius Valerius. *The Poems of Catullus*. Translated with an introduction by Peter Whigham. Berkeley: University of California Press, 1966.

Chapman, Morris H., compiler. *The Wedding Collection*. Nashville: Broadman Press, 1991.

Cherry, Kittredge, and Sherwood, Zalmon, ed. *Equal Rites: Lesbian & Gay Worship, Ceremonies and Celebrations*. Louisville: Westminster John Knox Press, 1995.

Ellmann, Richard, and O'Clair, Robert. *The Norton Anthology of Modern Poetry.* 2d ed. New York: W. W. Norton, 1988.

Fulghum, Robert. *From Beginning to End: The Rituals of Our Lives.* New York: Villard Books/Random House, 1995.

Gray, Amlin. *Kingdom Come.* New York: Theatre Communications, 1983.

Graziano, Marcheschi, and Seitz, Nancy. *Scripture at Weddings: Choosing and Proclaiming the Word of God.* Chicago: Liturgy Training Publications, 1992.

Grubbs, Judith Evans. *Law and Family in Late Antiquity: The Emperor Constantine's Marriage Legislation.* Oxford: Clarendon Press, 1995.

Horace, Quintus Horatius Flaccus. *The Complete Works of Horace.* Edited by Charles E. Passage. N.Y.: Fredrick Ungar Publishing, 1983.

Jewish Lights Publishing Staff. *How To Be a Perfect Stranger: A Guide to Etiquette in Other People's Religious Ceremonies.* Woodstock, N. Y.: Jewish Lights Publishing House, 1995.

Kahn, Cynthia. *Felix Hymenaeus: A Study of Greek and Roman Epithalamia through the Fourth Century A. D.* Ph. D. dissertation. Ann Arbor, Mich.: University Microfilms, 1991.

Kennedy, George. *The Art of Persuasion in Greece.* Princeton, N. J.: Princeton University Press, 1963.

———. *The Art of Rhetoric in the Roman World.* Princeton, N. J.: Princeton University Press, 1972.

Kramer, Ross Shepard. *Her Share of the Blessings: Women's Religions Among Pagans, Jews, and Christians in the Greco-Roman World.* New York: Oxford University Press, 1992.

Liturgikon. Indiana: Our Sunday Visitor, Inc., 1977.

Luther, Martin. *Luther's Works: The Christian in Society Vol. 1 # 44.* "A Sermon on the Estate of Marriage, 1519." Edited by James Atkinson. General Editor, Helmut T. Lehmann. Philadelphia: Fortress Press, 1966, 3–14.

———. *Sermons #1, Vol. 51,* "Sermon Preached at the Marriage of Sigismund von Lindenau in Merseburg, Heb. 13: 4, August 4, 1545." Edited and translated by John W. Doberstein. Philadelphia: Muhlenberg Press, 1959, 357–67.

Lutheran Book of Worship. Minneapolis: Fortress Press, 1978.

Martos, Joseph. *Doors to the Sacred: A Historical Introduction to Sacraments in the Catholic Church.* New York: Image Books, 1982.

McCullers, Carson. *The Member of the Wedding.* New York: Houghton Mifflin, 1946.

Menander Rhetor. Edited by D. A. Russell and N. G. Russell. Oxford: Clarendon Press, 1981.

Migne, Jacques-Paul, ed. *Patrologiae.* Series Graeca. Vol. 37. Paris: Migne, 1857.

Munro, Eleanor. *Wedding Readings: Centuries of Writing and Rituals on Love and Marriage.* New York: Viking Press, 1989.

Pfatteicher, Philip. *Commentary on the Occasional Services.* Philadelphia: Fortress Press, 1983.

Potts, James H. *Living Thoughts of John Wesley.* New York: Hunt & Eaton, 1891.

Rites of Marriage. New York: Catholic Book Publishing, 1970.

Rolvaag, Ole E. *Giants in the Earth: A Saga of the Prairie.* San Francisco: HarperCollins, 1965.

Rougemont, Denis de. *Love in the Western World.* Translated by Montgomery Belgion, 1940.

Rubenstein, Helen. *The Oxford Book of Marriage.* New York: Oxford University Press, 1990.

Sappho and the Greek Lyric Poets. Translated and annotated by Willis Barnstone. New York: Schocken Books, 1988.

Schillebeeckx, E., O. P. *Marriage: Human Reality and Saving Mystery.* Vols. 1 and 2. Translated by N. D. Smith. New York: Sheed and Ward, 1965.

Schleiermacher, Fredrich. *Servant of the Word: Selected Sermons of Fredrich Schleiermacher.* Translated with an Introduction by Dawn de Vries. Philadelphia: Fortress Press, 1987.

Selected Writings of C. F. W. Walther. Translated by Henry J. Eggold. Edited by Aug. R. Suelflow. St. Louis: Concordia, 1981.

Shideler, Mary McDermott. *The Theology of Romantic Love: A Study in the Writings of Charles Williams.* Grand Rapids, Mich.: Eerdmans, 1962.

Spong, John Shelby. *Living in Sin? A Bishop Rethinks Human Sexuality.* San Francisco: HarperSanFrancisco, 1988.

Stowe, Mrs. Harriet Beecher (under the pseudonym of Christopher Crowfield). *Little Foxes.* Boston: Ticknor and Fields, 1866.

The Book of Common Prayer. New York: The Church Hymnal Corporation, 1979.

The Rites of the Catholic Church. Vol. 1. New York: Pueblo Publishing Company, 1976.

Tufte, Virginia. *The Poetry of Marriage: The Epithalamium in Europe and Its Development in England.* University of Southern California Studies in Comparative Literature. Vol. 2. Los Angeles: Tinnon-Brown.

Uhrig, Larry J. *The Two of Us: Affirming, Celebrating and Symbolizing Gay and Lesbian Relationships.* Boston: Alyson Publications, 1984.

United Methodist Book of Worship. Nashville: United Methodist Publishing, 1992.

Willimon, William. *Worship as Pastoral Care.* Nashville: Abingdon Press, 1979.

Wilson, Paul Scott. *The Practice of Preaching.* Nashville: Abingdon Press, 1995.

Sermons

Acker, J. W., compiler. *Wedding Addresses.* Saint Louis: Concordia, 1955.

Burghardt, Walter J., S.J. "Christ and/or Buddha—Wedding Homily 4. *When Christ Meets Christ: Homilies on the Just Word.* Mahwah, N.J.: Paulist Press, 1993.

Gaiser, Fredrick J. "A Sign of Hope." *Christian Ministry* 21 (May/June 199): 29–30.

Niebuhr, H. Richard. "More Than Witnesses: A Wedding Homily." *Christian Ministry* 17/3 (May, 1986): 6–77.

Westerhoff, John H. "Homily Delivered on the Occasion of the Celebration and Blessing of the Marriage of Susan Bliss Emmons and Michael Lee Bentley." *Religion and Intellectual Life* 4 (Spring 1987): 105–6.

Sermon Collections

Augustine. *The Works of Saint Augustine: A Translation for the 21st Century.* Translated with notes by Edmund Hill, O. P. Edited by John E. Rotelle, O.S.A. New York: New City Press, 1990–95.

Burghardt, Walter J., S.J. *When Christ Meets Christ: Homilies on the Just Word.* Mahwah, N. J.: Paulist Press, 1993.

Donne, John. *The Sermons of John Donne.* Edited with Introductions and Critical Apparatus by Evelyn M. Simpson and George R. Potter. Vols. 1–10. Berkeley: University of California Press, 1953–1962.

Fant, Clyde E. Jr., and Pinson, William M., Jr., ed. *Twenty Centuries of Great Preaching.* Vols. 1–13. Waco, Tex.: Word Books, 1971.

Hoffsummer, Willi. *Of Wine in the Jars: Wedding Homilies.* Collegeville: Liturgical Press, 1995.

King, Horace Brown. *Together in Trust: Twenty-four Select Wedding Meditations.* Lima, Ohio: CSS Publishing, 1989.

Krueger, J. F., trans. and ed. *What God Hath Joined Together Let Not Man Put Asunder.* Burlington, Iowa: The Lutheran Literary Board, 1920.

Roses, Rings and Rejoicing: An Anthology of Selected Wedding Meditations from Parish Pastors. Lima, Ohio: CSS Publishing, 1990.

Sadler, William Alan, Jr., ed. *Master Sermons Through the Ages.* New York: Harper & Row Publishers, 1963.

Schaff, Philip, and Wace, Henry, eds. *A Select Library of Nicene and Post-Nicene Fathers of the Christian Church.* Second Series. New York: The Christian Literature Company, 1895.

This New Life Together: An Anthology of Wedding Meditations. Lima, Ohio: CSS, Publishing 1994.

Articles

Biddle, Percy. "The Wedding Sermon." In *A Concise Encyclopedia of Preaching.* Edited by William H. Willimon and Richard A. Lischer. Louisville: Westminster John Knox Press, 1995, 499–500.

Buttrick, David. "Preaching About the Family—The Candor and Concern of Biblical Faith." In *Preaching In and Out of Season.* Edited by Thomas G. Long and Neely Dixon McCarter. Louisville: Westminster/John Knox Press, 1990, 28–42.

Hastings, James, ed. "Marriage." In *Encyclopedia of Religion and Ethics.* Vol. 8. New York: Charles Scribner's Sons, 1916, 423–72.

Hendrix, Scott. "Masculinity and Patriarchy in Reformation Germany." *Journal of the History of Ideas, Inc.,* 56:2 (1995): 177–93.

Hughes, Robert. "Marriage Sermons As Ritual." *Academy Accents* 4:1 (April, 1988): 1–3.

Karant-Nunn, Susan C. "Kinder, Kuche, Kirche; Social Ideology in the Sermons of Johannes Mathesius." *Germania Ilustrata: Essays on Early Modern Germany Presented to Gerald Strauss*. Edited by Andrew C. Fix and Susan C. Karant-Nunn. Vol. 18. Series Sixteenth Century Essays & Studies, 1992, 121–40.

"Marriage." *Encyclopedia Judaica*. Vol. 2. New York: Macmillan and Jerusalem: Keter Publishing House, 1971, 1026–51.

"Marriage." *The Encyclopedia of Judaism*. Edited by Geoffrey Wigoder. Jerusalem: Jerusalem Publishing House, 1989, 461–67.

Oates, Wayne. "Preaching to Marriage and Family Needs." *Preaching* (January/February 1986): 13–15.

Wheeler, Arthur Leslie. "Tradition in the Epithalamium." *American Journal of Philology* 203: (June, 1930) 205–33.